Shrinking the SMIRCH

The Young People's edition

Life will never get better

SMIRCH-O-SHRINKER

PLEASE WAIT SHRINKING IN PROGRESS...

Jo Johnson

Illustrated by Lauren Densham

D1418889

Speechmark

Published in 2016 by

Speechmark Publishing Ltd
5 Thomas More Square, London E1W 1YW, United Kingdom
www.speechmark.net

002-6010/Printed in the United Kingdom by Hobbs

British Library Cataloguing in Publication Data

A catalogue record for this book is available from the British Library

ISBN: 978 1 90930 162 7

Acknowledgements

Many thanks to all the people who proof-read or gave constructive feedback on this book, namely Helen Taylor, Kaaren Wallace, Livvy Pinkney, Sue Duncan, Richard Johnson and Ruth Fischbacher. Their help has been invaluable in producing the finished product.

I would like to add a special thanks to Ben King, the Inclusion Manager at Steyning Grammar School, West Sussex. He generously gave of his time and effort in allowing me to try out smirch shrinking ideas on some of the pupils he supports. His help is very much appreciated.

In loving memory of Bethany Jupp, who loved all things creative and colourful.

Contents

A letter to explain the concept of a smirch and how it might help you. Here you can also meet eleven of the thirty young people who have shared their thoughts and feelings in this book.

This tells the imaginary story of the smirches, where they go to school, the textbook they read and the nasty tunes they play to make you think negative thoughts and have difficult feelings. This is the ONLY chapter that is a bit depressing as it seems like the smirch has all the power! Be sure to KEEP READING to find ways to shrink the smirch's power!

This chapter includes nine smirches that have been created by our team of young people. It also shows you their ideas for smirch equipment. This section encourages you to draw or imagine your own smirch (we all have one)!

This chapter includes three smirch shrinking tips to get you started on making life feel better. It helps you choose your values and the person you want to be. It also shows you how to set small goals and keep good records of what is happening in your life so you can catch out the smirch.

This chapter teaches you four ideas that will help everyone to feel less stressed.

Introduction

Dear Reader

I guess you might be wondering how a book with such an odd title can help you.

Do you have thoughts and feelings you would like to get rid of? Do you feel you don't fit in at school or at home? Do you wish you could change something about your appearance or personality? Do you wish you were more like other people? Do you often wonder what other people are thinking about you? Do you worry about how you look or that you will fail your exams Do you sometimes feel scared, sad or upset? Perhaps you feel you are the only one who has these thoughts and feelings. I can assure you that you are not.

Shrinking the smirch is about pretending those tricky thoughts and feelings are coming from an imaginary creature called a 'smirch'. Sounds like a strange idea, I know. Let me explain.

I think we all have a smirch, yes even you. I bet you have heard a lot about staying healthy: five a day, exercising, not taking drugs, that sort of thing. This is all about staying physically healthy and focusing on the body. Well, I think everyone should take a break from thinking so much about bodies and think more about minds. Shrinking the smirch is about the mind, what goes on in your head and coping with the pressure and challenges young people have to face at home and at school.

Perhaps when you were younger you had an imaginary friend. This workbook asks you to imagine that a smirch is a bad, unkind imaginary friend, the kind of friend who talks behind your back, pretends to be nice but really wants to put you down and bully you. It's a funsucker, it wants to take the fun and make you forget the good things in your life. The word smirch actually means a smudge. A smirch is something that perhaps makes you feel your life is not as good as it could be. A bit like black paint on your new designer T-shirt.

The idea of a bad imaginary friend probably sounds very strange but lots of clever people have used the idea of some sort of imaginary thing to help them feel better. I am sure you have heard of Winston Churchill. He was one of the most important people during the Second World War, but even he had a smirch! He was someone who experienced depression; this is when people feel really sad a lot of the time. He called his depression his black dog, a bad pet who set out to make his life miserable and lonely.

Many young people between 12 and 20 have helped us with this book and many of the ideas and pictures have been inspired by them. You can meet just a few of them on the next few pages. On pages 34-35 you can see some of their smirches. All the 'Blog Spots' are the private thoughts and feelings of other young people that they have kindly shared so you can see you are not alone. The smirch is a bully but 'Shrinking the smirch' gives lots of ideas about how you can beat this bully and cope better with all the thoughts and feelings that make you anxious and upset. I hope this workbook will show you how to keep your mind and your body healthy.

This book is not magic and just reading it won't help you. If you read a book about how to ride a bike but didn't get on a bike you would not learn how to cycle. 'Shrinking the Smirch' gives you lots of ideas that will help you feel better but only if you practise them in your life. The book is written in three parts. The first part helps you discover what your smirch is making you think, feel and do with exerpts from the smirch textbook. The second part invites you to imagine what your smirch might look like and understand the tricks it plays on you to ruin your day. The final part describes 20 things you can do to make your smirch as small as it can be so life feels more fun.

Best wishes with shrinking your smirch!

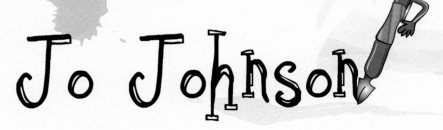

Jo Johnson

If you have purchased this book to help a young person you know...
they will gain most benefit if you first read it and understand the strategies so you can talk about what is in the book and offer support with practice.

If you are a parent...
the strategies will work best if as many family members as possible talk about and practise the ideas.

Meet some of our smirch-shrinkers...

Many young people have shared their thoughts and feelings to help you. Here are just a few of them

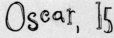

Oscar, 15

I live in Sussex with my parents and three siblings. My life is pretty good really but I worry a lot, I think probably more than other people. I worry about doing new things. I worry what people think of me and that they will think I am an idiot. I worry I will make mistakes. My smirch is called Lassey and my Mum has taught me some stuff to help me cope with my anxiety, and I realise that probably I will always worry more than some people.

Harriet, 13

I spend most of my time at boarding school but when I'm home, I live with my Mum, my sister and my cat. I am happy at school and at home most of the time. I get stressed quite easily and I tend to let people push me around a lot. I don't really fit in but I have an amazing group of friends with the same problem. Although I have two smirches, the one that affects me most is "Jessicatty" (see yearbook). I get angry and confused quite a bit.

Johanna, 17

I live with my sister and parents in West Sussex. I get anxious about talking to new people, even waiters in restaurants. I worry that people think I'm stupid or that I will say something wrong. My smirch is called Lippy and tells me that people are talking about me, which prevents me talking to new people.

Amber, 13

I live with my sister and Mum and Dad. I have recently started to worry and become more scared of many things. It's always the worst when I don't want it to be. Sometimes I feel like something is squeezing all the air out of me and I start to feel very sick and worried this is what my smirch army does. He always tries to make things difficult and I will probably always have armdy but I can face him and tell him to go away, and even though I do worry, I can always overcome it.

Ruby, 12

I have a sister, a mother and a father. I live in West Sussex. I go to School and do normal things. I worry quite a lot. I worry about small things like going on planes, being alone, having nobody to talk to and what I say. My smirch is called the "tummy butterfly" because when I'm really anxious, it sits on my tummy and gives me butterflies for a long time. I realise that I will still get anxious but also that there are ways I can help myself get better at overcoming my fears.

Tom, 13

Hi, my name is Thomas, I am 13 years old and live with my mum, dad and little brother. My mum has Multiple Sclerosis. My older brother is in the Navy. I am starting to worry more about myself, like how I look and what people think of me. My smirch lives in my school bag and whispers things to me during the school day, telling me I am not popular or no one likes me.

Katy, 18

I live with my parents. Until recently I didn't really realise I had a smirch but thinking about it, I do. I am a great worrier but my biggest fear of all is the fear of change. Whenever I face unknown situations I get anxious and worry about all the things that could go wrong. Until I was about 16 this prevented me from trying new things, but as I've got older my parents, teachers and friends have helped me overcome my smirch. So far I haven't been able to do it on my own but I hope as I get older change will get less frightening.

Leah, 13

I live with three older brothers. My family think I don't worry, but I think underneath I do worry but not as much as other people! I don't seem to have the need to look a certain way or do certain things, unlike my friends, as I like to be different and do things my way. When people are mean to me I have learnt to look them in the eye and answer back and then they don't really pick on me so much. Maybe having three brothers helps.

Matthew, 12

I live in Sussex with one brother and my parents. I have this thing where I have to clear my throat. Basically it limits me from doing certain activities. Mainly because I would be scared that I would need to clear my throat and then it would get worse and I would not be able to breathe, and then I would panic. I also worry that other people would see me doing it and then start doing it by being around me. This has happened a few times and caused me to have a panic attack. My smirch is called Koffin and because he makes me cough I then think I might die.

Katie, 17

I live in West Sussex with my parents and younger brother. I tend to worry a lot of the time and get easily stressed about exams and school work in particular, as well as sometimes feeling paranoid and anxious about what others think of me, which can mean that I hold back from fully being myself around people.

Genie, 14

I was born in Winchester. Every day I worry about lots of made up situations in my head. I worry that by now I should have found what I'm good at and know what I want to do with the rest of my life. I doubt myself so much and whenever I do feel confident I seem to mess things up. I'm not too bothered about what others think of me but sometimes I think I'm ugly and stupid.

Chapter 1: The Smirch Story

I know you are usually very mature and no longer believe in imaginary creatures, but are you willing to pretend just for this book that smirches are real? Yes? Ok then, in this chapter you can read all about smirches, where they go to school, what they learn and how they plan to upset and bully young people.

Once upon a time... (well all imaginary stories have to start with this, don't they?)

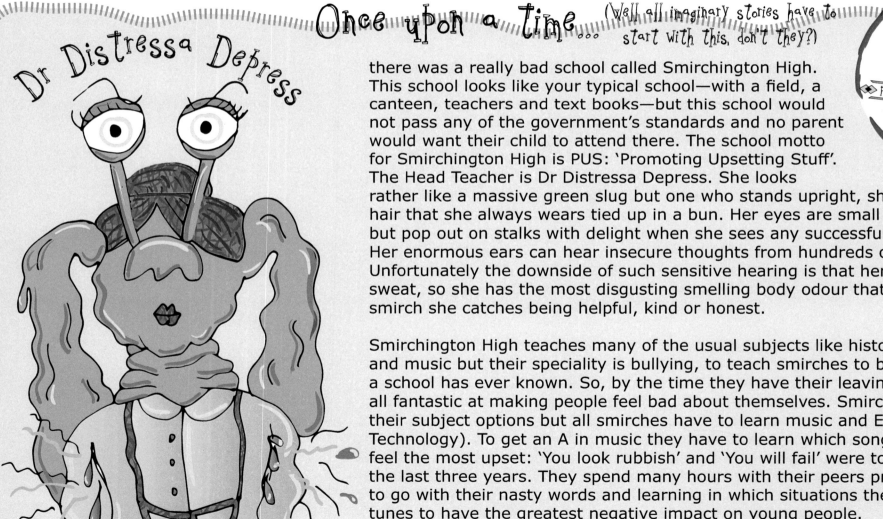

Dr Distressa Depress

there was a really bad school called Smirchington High. This school looks like your typical school—with a field, a canteen, teachers and text books—but this school would not pass any of the government's standards and no parent would want their child to attend there. The school motto for Smirchington High is PUS: 'Promoting Upsetting Stuff'. The Head Teacher is Dr Distressa Depress. She looks rather like a massive green slug but one who stands upright, she has grey hair that she always wears tied up in a bun. Her eyes are small and almost hidden but pop out on stalks with delight when she sees any successful acts of bullying. Her enormous ears can hear insecure thoughts from hundreds of miles away. Unfortunately the downside of such sensitive hearing is that her ears pour with sweat, so she has the most disgusting smelling body odour that she drips onto any smirch she catches being helpful, kind or honest.

Smirchington High teaches many of the usual subjects like history, English, art and music but their speciality is bullying, to teach smirches to be the best bullies a school has ever known. So, by the time they have their leaving prom they are all fantastic at making people feel bad about themselves. Smirches can choose their subject options but all smirches have to learn music and ET (Equipment Technology). To get an A in music they have to learn which song lyrics make people feel the most upset: 'You look rubbish' and 'You will fail' were top of the charts for the last three years. They spend many hours with their peers practising new tunes to go with their nasty words and learning in which situations they can play these tunes to have the greatest negative impact on young people.

PUS
PROMOTING UPSETTING STUFF
Working towards making young people miserable

ET Equipment Technology

ET is a class where the smirches learn how best to use their nasty equipment to upset people and make the world and other people look as horrid and scary as possible. Even the least academic smirches can do well in ET and no smirch is allowed to leave Smirchington High until they can efficiently use every piece of equipment. Check out the most popular pieces of smirch equipment on pages 31–33.

The only reason for living for a smirch is to stop young people from having any happiness in their lives and to make them do things that will hurt themselves or other people. Smirches work hard to keep humans so caught up with their own thoughts by playing them nasty songs that they can't enjoy the good things happening right in front of them. The gifted and talented smirches have extra lessons after school to teach them to spot the distressed and how to use their tools to cause the most sadness and pain.

Smirches all look very different. Some smirches have a definite human look. Other smirches resemble animals, whereas many don't look like anything that can be named. No two smirches are the same but despite their differences, they all do well in the same subjects. Check out a typical smirch school report on page 16. They are not evil, just irritating little fun sappers. Most of their time at smirch school is spent learning the Smirchington High rules which are all contained in a very heavy text book.

Smirches each have a Bag.

In their bag they keep their planner to tell them each day which young people will be best to pick on and what to use. They are drawn to people who they know might be easy to upset. Smirches know that a person will be an easier target if they are worried, sad or upset about something that has happened at home or at school, or if they are struggling to cope with life. On the next couple of pages, you can find things smirches keep in their bags.

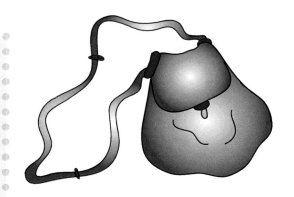

Smirch School Planner

Victim	Subject	Special info	Tune to play
Oscar Johnson	Maths	He has a test	You are rubbish at maths.
Kelly Myers	Throughout day	Parents are divorcing	Everyone will leave you. You are all alone.
Paul Briggs	On the bus	He is being bullied	No-one likes you.
Sammy Green	Breaktime	Had some new spots	You are so ugly. Everyone is looking at you.
Raj Faruk	Before P.E	He is a slow runner	No-one wants you on their team.
Simon Shelby	Throughout day	He is a carer for his disabled Mum	Your Mum will fall while you are out.
Cassie Melby	English and Maths	She has been seriously ill	You won't get better.

HOMEWORK

Make a long playlist of good songs to upset people who are worried about what they look like. Examples would be: 'you are ugly and fat' and 'you have to wear make up and a short skirt; everyone else is better looking.'

Due: Monday

Smirchington High Text Book

No smirch can leave Smirchington High without knowing everything in this book.

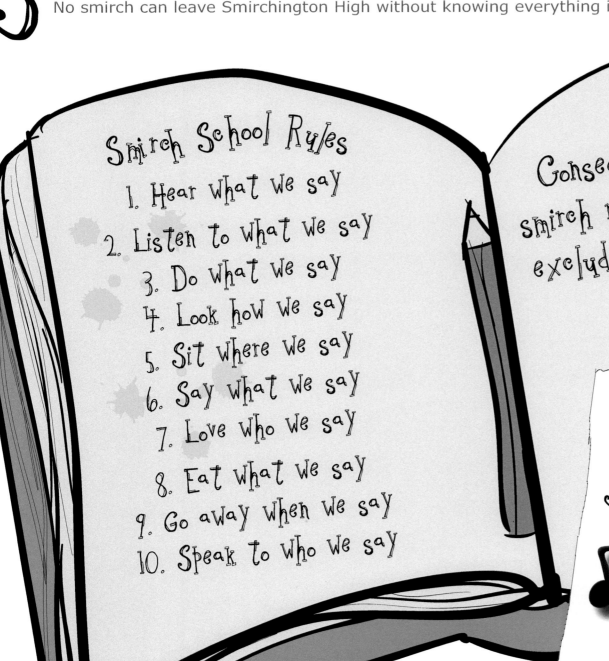

Smirch School Rules
1. Hear what we say
2. Listen to what we say
3. Do what we say
4. Look how we say
5. Sit where we say
6. Say what we say
7. Love who we say
8. Eat what we say
9. Go away when we say
10. Speak to who we say

Consequences if you disobey smirch rules: You will be ignored, excluded, unpopular and renamed as a loser

Smirch theme song
STOP, don't talk to me lamo, loser, wanna-be, like, oh totally!

I expect at your school or college they have a Behaviour Policy

The school policy probably includes things like this:
- You must show respect for property, teachers and other students.
- No verbal or physical aggression.
- No alcohol and drugs.
- No smoking.
- Be punctual for lectures.

Smirchington High also has a behavioural policy but Dr Depress would hate any humans to find out what is being expected of smirches so the school policies are all locked away in her office with her whip. An undercover journalist for *Not Ok* magazine has managed to get hold of a copy. They also found lots of hidden scientific articles about what makes young people feel better.

CONFIDENTIAL
Smirchington High
Behavioural Policy

A new term for your dictionary...

a **SMIRCHIN.** *noun*

This is a human being who helps smirches make people feel bad. They hang around in groups called 'IN' crowds and they help smirches by making other people feel pressured to do what they say, wear what they wear and go where they go. They make others feel so anxious about being left out that they push them into doing things to damage their bodies and minds. This book may also help you shrink the power of the smirchins.

Smirchington High Behavioural Policy

All smirches must follow these standards in order to upset as many young people as possible.

Behavioural Standard 1

Smirches must stop young people from finding out the following 'two life truths':

Truth A:

Thoughts, feelings and actions are very closely linked. Young people don't realise that what they think makes a big difference to how they feel and then that changes what they do, which changes how they think, and the loop goes on for ever. This loop is a smirch's best friend; if the humans start to see it clearly, they will notice the lyrics we are playing to them and stop listening.

Truth B:

Young people's brains are created in a way that makes them different. Humans love their pets so much that they think they function in the same way as people. Animals are creatures of habit who are selfish and stuck in their routines. Smirches must make sure that young people don't realise that they are not like animals but can think in a much more creative and rational manner and can learn new ways of thinking, feeling and acting. Keep them thinking they are similar to animals—who can't have faith, show respect, change the way they act or show kindness and respect to others—in order to make their health and relationships better.

Behavioural Standard 2

Humans are social beings; they are much happier and healthier when they spend time with others. This is not good for smirches as the humans get distracted and are less easily pulled into their thoughts by our songs.

Do everything you can to make young people stay on their own, hide under the duvet, pretend they are OK and give up anything they enjoy. If they are on their own a lot this will make them unhappy, unwell and stick to their destructive cycles of behaviour like shouting, harming themselves, over-eating and crying.

Prevent them from hearing about any science tips that might help them get healthier bodies or minds and tell them hundreds of lies to keep them in despair.

THE TRUTH ABOUT ALCOHOL

FACT
Alcohol makes you feel depressed.

YUM! DRINK THIS AND FEEL SO MUCH BETTER!

I agree to keep these standards.

Smirch signature .... Date ....

As in a regular school, smirches are issued with a termly report as shown on the right. They also have three main allergies so they have to carry a medical emergency ID card on them at all times like the one below.

Smirchington High School
School Report

Pupil: Smirchino   **Age:** 16   **Term:** Spring

SUBJECT	GRADE	COMMENT
Drama	A*	Smirches are all very good at drama and they try to create it wherever they can. They tell how others have failed so they will fall out. They love it when families split up as they know they will get lots of new ideas to create drama.
History	A*	Smirches are great at remembering all the embarrassing and upsetting things that have happened so they can remind young people of these things as much as possible.
I.T.	A*	Smirches love anything that involves technology. They make screens seem more interesting than people as they know this will keep people isolated and make it hard to sleep.
Art	A*	Smirches are excellent at art. They can make something that is very clear look very confusing. They are great at painting pictures in your head to make people feel scared, lonely and embarrassed.
Music	A*	Music is the best lesson of every smirch. They have the longest playlist in all the world and they know exactly the best time to play each tune. Just when you feel bad, they play the 'You have no friends' track and when you feel scared, they play 'You will fail.'
Community and Team Work	F	Smirches hate teams and friendships. They hate it when people help others, especially people who are less able or less popular. They love it when people are spiteful and unkind to themselves and others. They love it when people break up.
Health and Social	F	Smirches hate things that make people healthy in their minds and bodies. They make things like alcohol and drugs seem tempting and cool.

MEDICAL EMERGENCY ID CARD
Personal Information: smirch

ALLERGIES

The present
Smirches hate the here and now.

Kindness
Smirches also hate any act of kindness to self or others.

Good relationships
Smirches know that it is easier to get attention when young people are alone.

IF EXPOSED TO ANY OF THE ABOVE, SEEK MEDICAL HELP IMMEDIATELY OR USE SMIRCHIPEN TO INJECT ANTIDOTE OF EXTREME MISERY.

KEEP ON SMIRCH AT ALL TIMES

Chapter 1
Good Tunes for all situations

In this chapter you should find many of the situations young people face. Follow these four steps

1. When you see a young person, listen and watch until you find out what they are struggling with.

2. Look up the situation and write the most useful tunes in your planner to play when needed.

3. Make a note of which songs cause the most distress so you can play them time and time again.

4. If you can't find the exact situation, try some songs from other situations and see what works best in making young people feel upset, sad or angry.

On the next page, you will find a selection of good songs to play in different situations. You can add these to your Bag to use at a moment's notice. See example Below:

Situation

New School or new set?

No one will like you, you won't fit in, you will have no friends, you are stupid, everyone thinks you are too thick, everyone thinks you are too clever

Lyric ideas

New School or new set?

'No one will like you, you won't fit in, you will have no friends, you are stupid, everyone thinks you are too thick, everyone thinks you are too clever.'

Puberty?

'Your body is disgusting, everyone is staring, your body is too small, your body is too big, look at the state of you, look in the mirror.'

Family life changing/ divorce/ separation/ someone has died or left home?

Everyone will leave, it's your fault, you are not the favourite, you cause all the trouble, your life is rubbish, everyone else has a happy home, no one wants you, no one understands.'

Spots/ weight gain/ weight loss/ Bad haircut/ wrong uniform/ unfashionable/ Body hair/ disability?

'Your body is so awful, everyone is looking at you, you are so fat and ugly, you are so thin and ugly, you are not good enough, you are not popular, look at the state of you, you are so weird, you make me feel sick, why are you alive?'

Different home life/ different culture/ family go to church/ living with grandparents/ in care/ young carer?

'Everyone thinks you are weird, no one likes you, what would they think if they knew, you are a loser, run away, it's your fault, you are not good enough.'

In trouble?

'You are so bad, you will always fail, the teachers hate you, your parents don't want you, your parents are so disappointed, don't bother trying, give up, run away.'

Gifted and talented?

'No one likes you, losers are clever, clever people are ugly geeks, you will fail, give up.'

Ill health?

'You won't get better, it's your fault, why me? Your parents blame you, it's only you, no one understands, you will get so behind, everyone will forget you.'

Finding School Work too hard?

'You are stupid, everyone is laughing, your parents are disappointed, you will never get to college, you will be unemployed, no one likes you, you are not good enough.'

Chapter 2

Messing with heads

Rule 1: Make sure young people spend as much time as possible tangled up in their heads with all their thoughts and fears so they don't enjoy life.

Rule 2: Play songs constantly with nasty lyrics to distract young people from whatever they are doing. (Lots of good ideas for songs in Chapter 1.)

Rule 3: Remind young people of all the bad things that have happened to them, make them think about all the scary things that could happen in the future.

The very best smirch equipment to mess with heads

Smirchigoggles

Invisible goggles to make the world and everything in it look rubbish—a rubbish body, a rubbish job—even closest family are not good enough when viewed by these glasses. They are so transparent that the humans don't notice the goggles are changing the view.

A Smirchipod

This very small device holds the longest playlist with hundreds of different tunes chosen to be as upsetting as possible. The most popular tunes are listed in Chapter 1 of this book. The top ten songs in the smirch charts last year were: 'You will fail', 'Everyone hates you', 'You have no real friends', 'You are not good enough', 'You look ugly', 'What are they saying about you?' 'Loser, loser, loser', 'Something bad will happen', 'It's your fault' and 'Nothing will change'. Thoughts and worries are what human beings call these songs in their heads. All smirches can use a smirchipod very well.

Imagine a magic USB stick that could be plugged into heads to measure how much time you are concentrating on what you are doing and how much time you are listening to your thoughts and smirch songs in your head. If this information was then downloaded and displayed in a bar chart, what would yours look like? If you are like most people, it would look like the picture on the right.

Time spent in head

Time spent paying attention

Typical young person's thinking pattern

Most people (yes, adults as well) spend heaps of time paying attention to what is going on in their heads. Some people use phrases like 'away with the fairies', 'head in the clouds' or being 'on autopilot' to describe what we all do a lot of the time, thinking, worrying, planning, remembering and panicking. These things are all thoughts and pictures in your head. We describe them as fears, ideas, plans and attitudes but they are just random words. Mostly they are not helpful words but unkind, angry and frightening.

Smirches love the fact that you listen really hard to the thoughts playing in your head, believing it all, as if it is a real life documentary on what has happened or what is going to happen in the future. They know if they throw in a short video clip it will make you even more likely to listen to the words in your head.

They want you to listen more and more to the playlist in your head as they know that when you are listening to their songs you are not thinking about the delicious food you are eating, you are not enjoying talking to a funny friend, following the story in the book or understanding your teacher.

Smirches know how easy it is to distract you with a thought:

A thought about home

'It's all going wrong.'
'They don't understand.'
'I hate them.'

A thought that you are not as good as others

'What do you look like?'
'Look how thin she is.'
'He is so much more popular than you.'

A negative thought about your performance

'Well you messed that up.'
'Failed again, loser.'
'Everyone is laughing at you.'

What are they thinking about you?

'Did you see how he looked at you?'
'She thought you were an idiot.'

The smirches know that most of the time young people don't even notice the songs that are playing in their heads or that they are believing the words as if they are being spoken by a good friend. Smirches find it strange that young people don't realise they are feeling upset, sad or angry because of the lyrics they are listening to rather than what is actually happening.

Young people often don't realise everyone is the same; they worry that they are the only person who has bad thoughts and pictures going on in their heads. You might have tried to get rid of these words and pictures but that just makes the smirches laugh as they know it's hopeless. The words and pictures come back and the harder you try to get rid of them, the louder the smirches turn up their smirchipods adding some new lyrics like: 'you are so weird', 'no one else has thoughts like that', 'what would people think of you?' and 'your smirch is always going to win'.

Smirches just love the fact that such struggles take up SO much energy and make you feel so horrible!

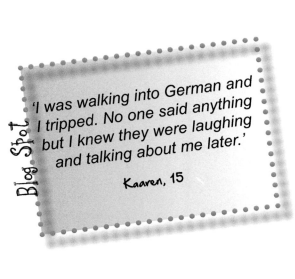

Blog Spot

'I was walking into German and I tripped. No one said anything but I knew they were laughing and talking about me later.'

Kaaren, 15

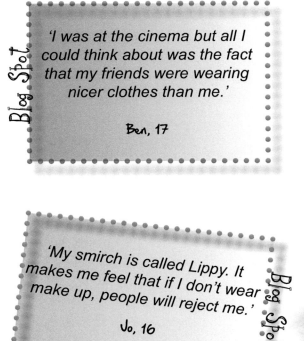

Blog Spot

'I was at the cinema but all I could think about was the fact that my friends were wearing nicer clothes than me.'

Ben, 17

'My smirch is called Lippy. It makes me feel that if I don't wear make up, people will reject me.'

Jo, 16

Blog Spot

You have heard the same lyrics time and time again But you still keep listening to the popular tunes of

You are not welcome.
You will fail.
Everyone will leave.
What will people think?
You are not normal.
It's not worth trying.
You are not good enough.
Life will never get better.
No one likes you.
They are talking about you.
You are going to get ill.
Loser! Loser! Loser!

Chapter 3
Aims for feelings

Aim 1: Young people must be made to believe that all others are free of bad feelings.

Aim 2: Make young people believe that painful feelings are bad and avoidable and only happen to the weak.

Aim 3: Don't let the young people realise that the bad feelings are a result of the thoughts and pictures we play them.

Essential smirch equipment to impact feelings

Adrenalin Pill

This makes big changes inside your body that makes the heart rate increase, your blood pressure go up and your body sweat. This can make you feel shaky, weak or sick and even confused, and often makes people feel like they want to run away or fight.

Smirchiscope

Makes you focus on small feelings and body sensations until the feelings and sensations are all you can think about.

Smirchiplayer

This plays films of all your embarrassing and bad memories as well as films about all the things that you worry might happen in the future. Smirches know that humans recognise what they play as memories or mental images. Smirches know that for the best impact this needs to be used together with a Smirchipod to create pictures and words at the same time.

Smirchinks

All smirches are given a set of syringes when they leave school to use with different coloured inks:
Red to make you angry.
Yellow to make you feel sick.
Black to give a sense of doom and darkness.

SMIRCHINKS

Smirches need you to believe that everyone else is happy and free of negative emotions such as anger, sadness, fear or anxiety. Smirches play you images of other people's bodies, families, relationships and possessions. The images are air-brushed so they look much better than they really are. At the same time they like to wind you up with songs about how your appearance is not good enough and how you always fail and look stupid. They play these songs at the same time as images of all your friends at parties or having fun with their wealthy, fun families. They want you to feel that if only you had a new body or a better brain or a different family you would be free of all your bad feelings.

Imagine you have made a small mistake, you notice someone looking at you or you remember a lost friend or a bad memory. Smirches rub their hands together because they know your brain will notice this minor problem before you do and will make your stomach lurch.

All the smirches then have to do is play one of their nasty songs:

You are feeling Bad.
It can only get Bigger.
Why always me?
You are so Weak.
Everyone knows.
You are going to cry.
You will never Be happy again.

24

This Bad feeling quickly grows

Smirches know bad feelings like fear, anxiety, low mood and sadness have no power. They love bad feelings though and do everything they can to make people feel bad. They know young people hate feeling like this and how much they will panic and struggle when the bad feelings start. The smirches know that they will then get all caught up in their thoughts again and try and hide or ignore their feelings. Smirches know that struggling and panicking about these feelings makes them worse and worse. The smirches find this hilarious to watch as they know then that the person will do unhealthy things to try and feel better like drink too much, overeat or shout at the people they love.

The smirches know that this cycle of struggling and then the unhealthy habits make all the bad feelings stronger and come more often. When a young person gets caught up in this cycle they know that their work is done for the day. It always surprises them how gullible humans are as it only takes a small mistake, an odd look or a bad memory to get all this action going.

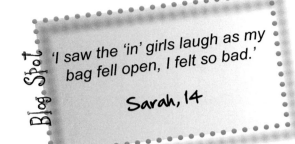

Blog Spot

'I saw the 'in' girls laugh as my bag fell open, I felt so bad.'

Sarah, 14

Blog Spot

'I feel so sad about my life. Nothing makes me feel better apart from smoking weed but then I feel worse as I can't control anything.'

Lee, 17

'I can feel my stomach starting to churn and I panic I will be sick, I get redder and redder as I know people can see how weird I am.'

Karen, 14

Blog Spot

'Sometimes I feel so bad that I feel like life is not worth living.'

Hugo, 14

Blog Spot

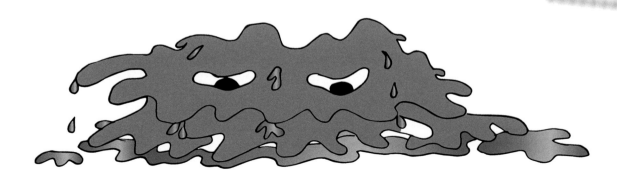

Chapter 4

Aims for Behaviour

Aim 1: Make sure young people don't get closer to who or what they would like to be or what they would like to achieve.

Aim 2: Make sure they hurt the people they want to have in their lives.

Aim 3: Make sure they do things that will make them feel worse.

Aim 4: Make sure they do lots of things to try and get rid of bad feelings.

Essential smirch equipment to change Behaviour

Urge Pill

So that you can't think of anything else but a certain urge. These urges are always negative and will take you further away from the life you want. The urge might be to overeat, drink too much, withdraw, shout at your family or harm yourself.

URGE PILLS

Blog Spot

'I had a really bad morning at home. When I got to school my teacher said my coat should be off. I threw a chair at him and got suspended. Sometimes I hate myself so much.'

Fred, 16

Blog Spot

I was out with my parents when I realised I hadn't put any make up on. I felt sick and really afraid I would bump into people who knew me. I know I ruined the day for everyone, which made me feel so rubbish and stupid.'

Jo, 16

Smirches know the power starts with the thoughts and the lyrics. They know that soon the bad feelings will follow without them having to do much at all. Smirches know that when the bad feelings come, they just need to plant a negative thought and soon you will be doing something to make everything worse. Smirches are masters at using all their skills together to make you do things you don't like. They love it when you feel so bad that you are easy to manipulate into doing what they want. They can then make you angry and you are soon shouting at your friend or parents when it wasn't really their fault, or they make you sad and you eat too much or harm yourself.

They love it when you start to feel so bad that you stay by yourself or avoid doing what you really want to do.

At this point they play you some of their favourite tunes

Loser loser loser.

You are an epic fail.

There is no point in trying.

You have done it again.

You have spoilt it.

You are not good enough.

Everyone is laughing at you.

They are now happy, the negative circle is complete.

They can wind you up with their nasty lyrics and bad memories, then they know you will soon be feeling terrible. Then off you will go, doing things that they know take you further away from your values and make you unhealthy.

Hooray, their job for the day is done. Now their chosen young person is unable to do anything positive and won't experience any good feelings.

They can just leave them with a final lyric, or four:

It's down, down, down.

Why do you even try?

Fail, fail, and fail.

You are just not good enough.

27

So, where are we going now?

In this section you get to have a look at other people's smirch related ideas and create your own. Have fun!

Smork

He makes me feel rubbish.

He has orange and green fur and sits on my shoulders weighing me down.

The Bully in your head

So have you got the idea from the smirch school report and textbook? The smirch is just a bully in your head. It is your personal enemy. It says very upsetting things to hurt you and wind you up. Your smirch wants to watch you fall into the pit of despair as it knows that when you are in there you will do things that are not good for your body or mind and then everything will feel worse.

Everyone has different things that they do when the smirch gets them in the pit. Some people eat too much, others starve themselves, some hurt themselves, others hurt others, some drink too much alcohol or use substances to make themselves forget, whilst others just withdraw and hide away. The smirch loves these things as it knows they all make you stop being yourself.

So it's like a lot of the time you and the smirch are in a tug of war with a pit of anxiety and despair (as a big black hole) in the middle. When you listen to what the smirch is saying, believe it and do things to keep it happy, it gets bigger and stronger and you are more likely to fall into the pit.

Shrinking the smirch is about learning how to let go of the rope. The smirch will always be there saying nasty things to make you feel bad, but it will have lost its fight with you. If you stop pulling your end of the rope, the smirch will get weaker and smaller and its voice will become easier to ignore. If you are willing to learn, this workbook will show you how to notice the smirch and its pull on you. It will also show you how to find ways to ignore this bully in your head by paying attention to other things so you can do the things in life you enjoy and be more like the person you want to be.

If that sounds tempting keep reading....

This section allows you to think about what your personal smirch is like.

There are some ideas from other people to make you think, but every smirch is different as each person and their situation is unique.

When you have looked at the ideas of others and read about the range of smirch equipment you can perhaps draw or glue a picture of your smirch in the space provided on page 37.

Some people find it easier to create their smirch out of other materials like plasticine, paper mâché or even fabric. You might want to do it by yourself, with a group of friends or with your family.

You might want to use this section to talk to others about the struggles your smirch creates for you. If you can talk about your smirch and its nasty little ways, you will be taking a big step towards stopping the tug of war and shrinking your smirch.

The smirch shown on the right was drawn by Georgina, age 14

Patronising tone of voice but shouts when I get things wrong

Wears armour so I can't fight away bad thoughts

Claws to make anything bad that happens worse and more painful

Has wings representing my goals and ambitions that I can't seem to make take flight

Achieves everything I can't

Beautiful so makes me feel ugly and unwanted

Always smiling, laughing at all I do, making me feel stupid and insignificant

Always watching me to see if I can live up to my high expectations

Equipped with lots of tools so she can get to me in both expected and unexpected ways

EQUIPMENT USED BY SMIRCHES

Some smirch equipment has already been revealed in the textbook. Here are some other smirch gadgets available for them to buy at Smirchistore Direct. Some of the gadgets have been designed by our team of young people.

SmaceBook

This is a magic book that smirches can switch on in your mind to show you other people's lives: the fun they are having, the great friends they have, the places they have been and how popular they are. It is used when you are alone and feeling sad. The smirch switches on the book like a screen in your head and flicks through page after page so you feel insecure and lonely.

By Kaaren, 15

SmirchairBrush

The smirches all have an air brush. They can use it on videos, magazines and real people. It makes the people and images you look at perfect in every way so that you feel you are not good enough.

Smirchicam

These send smirchisnaps: instant pictures that have the power to ruin a good moment just by a flash picture. The pictures will always be of someone else looking more happy, fit and popular than you.

By Jo, 16

Smirchilever

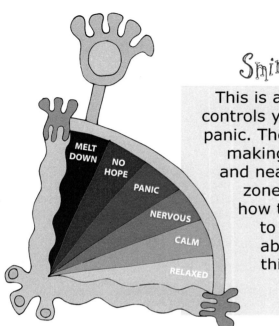

This is a lever which controls your feelings of panic. The smirch enjoys making it get nearer and nearer to the black zone by telling you how things are going to go wrong and about all the bad things that could happen.

By Oscar, 12

Word machine

This is a bit like a lottery gadget, but instead of throwing out numbers, it throws out random words, smells or pictures. The words can be a label such as bad, fat, loser, ugly or the name of a person or place that has the power to remind of fears or something bad that has happened. Smells can be a familiar scent that arouses a powerful memory—pictures of a face or a classroom. This works well with humans. The smirches know that just the right thing thrown out at the right time and place can pull you up into your head and make you think and panic.

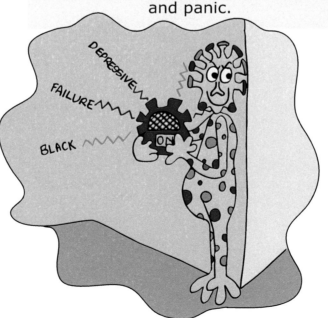

Smirchilighter

Smirches have lighters that light tempers. They use them when you are most stressed or unhappy. They want you to shout at your friends so they get upset and feel uncomfortable around you.

By Harriet, 13

Smirchivids

The tiniest DVD cassettes that can be linked to the smirchiplayers. Only a few smirches have them. They are used with the right lyrics and images to create films and sounds to remind you of when something upsetting, embarrassing or frightening happened. They can record their nasty little films so that when you see or hear things that are similar, your mind and body feel as if the real thing is happening again.

Fatigue pipe

This is a pipe that can be plugged into your finger when you are sleeping. People need a full tank of energy to deal with life. The fatigue pipe can be used to suck out your energy so that you wake up the next day with so little energy that even getting up feels draining and by mid-morning you are truly shattered.

Smutterfly Net

This is a net with really small holes so nothing can escape. Smirches use smutterfly nets to catch butterflies when they see young people trying to do something really important. They put the net behind someone and it makes them feel like they have butterflies moving around in their bodies.

By Ruby, 12

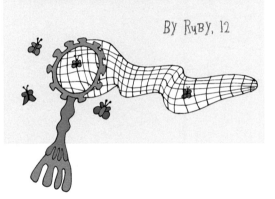

Smirchiphones

These are headphones that fit perfectly with a smirchipod. They are constantly set to the highest volume and make all the negative smirch lyrics play really loudly so you can't hear what is going on around you. They make the negative smirch ideas even louder and they can also be used to make you imagine you hear things people are saying which aren't true like, "she's ugly' and weird", or "he's a loser".

By Tom, 12

Kerfuzzel Spray

Smirches use this spray to kerfuzzel all your ideas so you can't think very well and your head feels muddled and confused. They are using this when you need to answer a question in class or if you are in an exam.

Smirchilenses

These are daily contact lenses, but rather than making the world appear clearer they impair vision in some way. They can make the world seem darker or scarier than it actually is. They can make you see things which are not real or make you imagine people are staring and laughing at you when they're not.
They make others look better in every way but when you look at yourself they emphasise all the things you hate, both inside and out.

CONTACT LENSES

Panic Button

Most smirches know that panic buttons are best used with an adrenalin pill, some black ink and when smirchipods are on fast forward, so lyrics are jumbled and fast. As soon as the panic button is noticed, it makes a person feel overwhelmed by their symptoms, which usually makes them put up a fight to try and push away their symptoms, or to avoid the situation they are in from then on. Smirches all know that if they can use panic buttons as much as possible people will soon be staying in to avoid other people and their lives will shrink whilst the smirches' power will grow.

PANIC

All the smirches shown here have been created by young people

Brain Bowl

'This smirch stops positive thinking and stirs bad thoughts or memories.'

Bag smirch

'This two headed smirch lives in my backpack and comes to school with me every day. It whispers in my ears that I'm not good enough, good looking enough or popular enough.'

Lassey

'My smirch has a rope (lasso) to make your body feel tight, red ink to make your head hot and a feather to tickle your tummy to make it feel jittery.'

Lippy

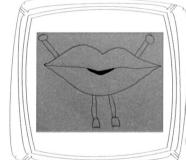

'This smirch makes me feel like I'm not good enough and that I'll always have to look good and wear make up or I will be rejected.'

Firehands

'A scarey hot smirch that makes me sweat and panic until I feel like I might throw up.'

Koffin

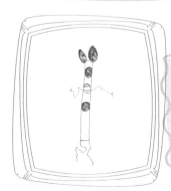

'This smirch makes me feel like I can't breathe and makes me cough, and then I think I might die or make other people cough too.'

Jessicatty

'This smirch is always there to make me angry. She has no mouth but her silence seems to whisper uncertainty in my ear. She is partly made of fire to set off my temper and her eyes are hollowed out to scare me. Her imagination is represented by a third eye and it corrupts my thoughts into hate and anger.'

Belladonna

'This smirch loves making me feel like I'm not good enough. Her make up, perfect hair and her latest trendy clothes make me feel ugly, whilst her stick thin body makes me feel fat. She is two-faced and somehow tells everyone my secrets. Her claws stab me in the back and her fangs leave emotional scars. Her eyes intimidate me and stop me seeking help from others.'

Lactatio

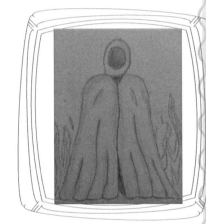

'It has no real features, but it is simply there, and always there. It has no mouth yet it speaks to me and tells me that whatever I'm doing won't work. It tells me people will laugh and think I'm stupid. This smirch can make me panic at the smallest things and is at its strongest when a teacher looks round the class about to pick on someone. It says they will choose me and I will not answer correctly and I will look bad and even the teacher will laugh if I try to answer. This smirch makes me panic everytime I don't know the answer.'

You can look at the smirches described by other people but your smirch will be unique.

Use these questions to help you think about what your smirch would look, feel and sound like if it was not an imaginary bully in your head but a real creature.

My smirch

What colour and pattern does it have?
Just one colour, stripes or spots?

What are its favourite tricks and equipment?

What does it look like?
Does it have animal features?
Does it look like a person?
Does it have ears? If so how many?
Does it have eyes? If so how many?
Are its eyes on stalks, on the back of the head or on its toes?

What does its voice sound like or is it silent?

What kind of bag does it have to carry its accessories: a sack, a carrier bag, a hand-made satchel?

Which thoughts/lyrics do you often hear?
You are rubbish.
You will fail.
It won't work.
Stay in.
What are they thinking?
You are not good enough.
It's happening again.
They think I am weak.
No one likes me.
What will they say?
My parents are rubbish.
Everyone else is better.
It can only get worse.
I am a burden.
People pity you.

What would it feel like if you could touch it?
Is it slimy, spiky, smooth or rough?

What shape is it?
Is it tall?
Is it round? Is it small?

Which pictures and films does it always play?
Childhood memories.
The school bully.
The past failures.
Everyone else's happy life.
You sick and ill.
You on your own.
You gaining weight.

Draw your smirch here or write a description

Name

Brief description

So do you have a picture of this smirch Bully in your head?

Some people find it hard to come up with a picture so you might just want it to have a name. If you are willing you could ask your family or even friends if they have any ideas about what a smirch might look like or be named. Ask them about their smirches.

Who can be your real or imaginary supporters?

Everyone needs a smirch shrinking supporter to help them defeat these creatures. After all Batman has Robin, Dr Who always has a helpful assistant, Sherlock has Dr Watson and Wonder Woman has Wonder Girl.

Who will help you stand up to this smirch Bully?

So what will you choose?

- A cuddly teddy bear that comes alive when needed?
- A perfect imaginary friend who makes no demands?
- A beautiful flower or tree that speaks kind words?
- A pet like a kitten or puppy that is warm? Or someone else?
- A super story robot?

Maybe you can think of a real friend or family member who will support you to shrink the smirch. Perhaps you can share your goals and plans with them as you try some of the ideas in this book. If someone who was helpful to you is no longer alive, you can still think of them as your supporter and imagine what they would have said and done to encourage you. If you have a living faith in God, then He is always on your side.

Will you have any tools or gadgets to help you?

- A remote control that turns off the smirchipod and player?
- An antidote for his pills?
- A liquid to change the colour of his inks?
- A lead to control the smirch?
- A shield to defend you against the generating machine?

So we all have a smirch.

Smirches are a bit like children, some cause more trouble than others! Your smirch will be with you all your life but there will be times when it is much louder. Smirches often feel stronger when you have tricky things to cope with like exams, friendship troubles or family problems.

So if you can't get rid of your smirch you need to think about a way of living with it but not fighting and struggling with it. The fighting, trying to ignore it or doing negative things to try and shut it up takes so much energy and doesn't help. You could be using that energy to have fun and do things that will help you and others.

In chapter 1 we thought about how smirches are good at being a bad influence and bullying you, but...

- **Can you see that some of your distress and anxiety is due to the struggle you are having with the smirch and the effort you are using to keep the smirch quiet and hidden?**

- **Can you see that there are perhaps small things that are in your control that you could change?**

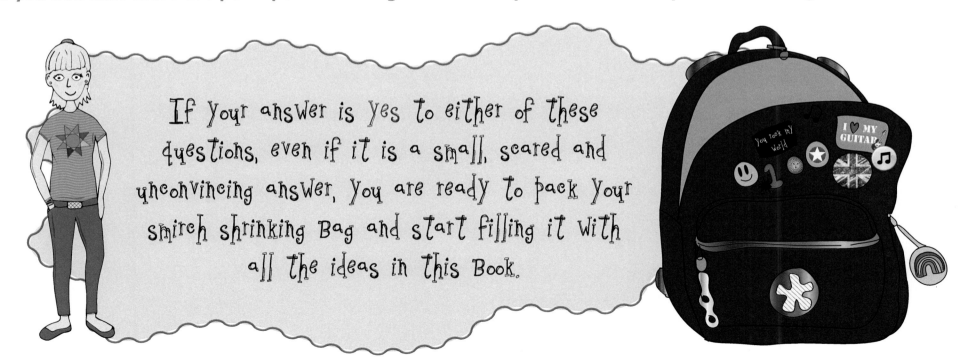

If your answer is yes to either of these questions, even if it is a small, scared and unconvincing answer, you are ready to pack your smirch shrinking Bag and start filling it with all the ideas in this Book.

This will not make your smirch happy.

Your smirch wants you to stay feeling helpless and insecure so it was hoping you would not open this book. Now you have opened it, the smirch is already shrinking, but smirches are like other insecure people, the worse they feel, the more they say spiteful things.

The smirch is feeling insecure so it is playing you these songs on its smirchipod:

What if others knew you were reading this?
You are so weird!
Everyone else can cope.
How ridiculous.
This is for mental people.
Nothing helps you.

The smirch needs you to feel defeated so it plays a film in your head of:

The time you failed.
You on your own.
You shouting at your parents.
You having a panic attack.

Your smirch shrinking Bag

If the smirch has a big bag of ideas to annoy and upset you, it's only fair that you have a bag too.

Bags are very important to young people; everyone must have the right kind of bag. Here is an opportunity for you to create an imaginary bag that can be as expensive as you like and any style or colour. What will your bag be like? It needs to be a great bag that you can feel proud to carry and it needs to be strong enough to hold all the shrinking tips and equipment that you will gather to shrink your smirch.

What will You choose?

A rucksack?

A colourful Bag with lots of accessories?

A satchel?

A smart Brief case?

As you go through this workbook you will read about different things you can do to help yourself feel better and make your smirch feel smaller. Each shrinking tip gives you one idea to put in your imaginary bag. You might want to draw your chosen bag so you can imagine filling it with lots of ideas that work to shrink your smirch.

You might like some of the ideas but others won't be what you need. Some skills will be useful some of the time but at other times they won't work. As you get to know your smirch and its games you will get better at noticing what is making life difficult and knowing what works best and in which situations.

Draw your smirch shrinking Bag Below

Type of Bag ....

Colour ....

Accessories ....

SCIENCE FACT

CONFIDENTIAL **TOP SECRET** CONFIDENTIAL

In this workbook you will find the 'leaked' science tips from the recent raid of Dr Depress's office that have been published by Notok magazine. You can be assured that what the smirches were hiding will work to make you feel better, so pay attention.

Get ready to fill your empty bag with 20 smirch shrinking strategies!

RESOURCES PACKED

43

Shrinking tip 1
Decide Who You Want to Be

A really odd question?

Who are you and is it who you want to be?

Adults often put pressure on young people to do what they think are good ideas. They say:

Work harder

Don't work so hard

Get a flat

Eat more

Drink less

Blah blah blah!

Get a degree

Go to college

Get good grades

Avoid that friend

Go to the doctor

Be a doctor

Many of these things are good ideas but they are all things to **DO** and you are a human being not a human doing!

From a young age you have probably been asked what you want to do when you grow up. Has anyone asked, who do you want to be? It is easy to grow up knowing what you want to **DO** or what others want you to **DO** but still not knowing who you want to **BE**.

What would happen if you and a group of friends set out to go to a party without knowing where you were going? You would get lost, waste loads of time, feel frustrated, shout at each other, be late, feel worried and upset.

Growing up without deciding who you want to be or what is important to you is like setting off without knowing how to get there or where you are going. The results are the same: you get anxious and frustrated, you get lost, arguments happen and you waste lots of time on things that are not important.

Maybe if you could get an idea about **who you want to BE** this might help you think about the direction you need to take.

It would also help you to know when you are on the right path but also when you are on the wrong path.
We are talking about **VALUES.**

Values

1) Who you want to be.
2) What's really important to you.
3) The things that would matter if no one else was around.
4) **Values are not** goals.

Goals

Goals are things you can tick off as finished such as get a B in maths, get a job or buy a car. Goals are important but values are more important. They are what you want to be like as a person whatever you are doing, whoever you are with, whatever you look like and whatever things you have.

Knowing Your values...

will help you decide whether what you are thinking, feeling or doing at any moment is in line with who you want to be or not.
So how do you find out what your values are? Here are four ideas; see which one works best for you:

Idea 1: It's your party...

Imagine it's your 18th, 21st or 30th birthday party. Only people you love and respect are there. Someone has been asked to make a truthful speech about what you are really like. What would you like them to say? Don't think about the superficial stuff like appearance or even your abilities, but who you want to be as a person and what is really important to you.
See an example of a speech about a smirch on the next page...

Smirch values

Dishonest

Shallow

Focused on looks

Unkind

Two-faced

Unfaithful

Ungrateful

Unhealthy

Angry

Rude

Dirty

Lazy

A smirch Birthday speech

'I have known this smirch for many years. He always blames others and he wants each one of you to feel it's your fault. He wants you to worry about all the nasty things he can do to you. He loves to make people afraid, hurt, angry or scared. He tries to always be spiteful, dishonest, unkind and cruel.

He loves to think only of himself and to be sure you are thinking about him too. He loves to make others feel they can only do what he says, they can only wear what he allows and look as he says. He likes to remind people of what they haven't got and when they are failing and he hates it when people do anything to make their bodies or minds feel better. He loves it when people are alone and does everything he can to cause splits and arguments and tries to make as many people as possible shout and hurt others.

He likes to be as unpredictable as possible and is a two-faced, back-biting creature who hates it when people notice what he is up to.'

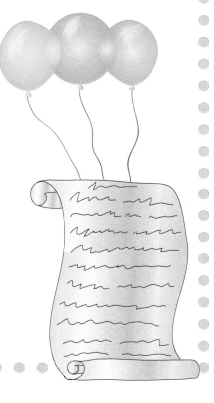

Smirch lie

Don't bother with all this stuff. Being honest and kind won't make you feel better.

A new term for your dictionary...

a **SMIRCH SHRINKER.** *noun*

This is a human who is the opposite to a SMIRCHIN. A smirch shrinker has taken the time to think about who they want to be and have decided to be as healthy as possible by noticing what is going on.

Idea 2: Ask yourself what qualities would make a good friend...

'A good friend should always support you and not let you down in any situation. I think they should be someone that you can fully trust with anything, knowing that they'll have your best interests at heart. They should also be someone that you feel comfortable around and can joke about with.'

Katie 17

'A good friend would be sure to have your back when you need it and to always help you. A good friend needs to be someone that cares about you and will be there for you in all situations and will never leave you behind. They don't care what you look like but they like you for who you are on the inside.'

Melissa 17

'A good friend respects you and is not judgmental because everyone's different and you should respect each other's opinions. Loyalty is important too. I like people who are considerate and in a good mood most of the time, not grumpy all the time. I would like them to be funny, not comical but able to take a joke.'

Harry, 15

Idea 3: Look at what someone else has written...

Have a look at this excerpt from The Message version of the Bible as it gives a good summary of what most of us would like our values to be. It might sound familiar as it gets read at lots of weddings.

*'Love never gives up.
Love cares more for others than for self.
Love doesn't want what it doesn't have.
Love doesn't boast, doesn't have a big head, doesn't force itself on others, isn't always "me first", doesn't fly off the handle, doesn't keep score of the wrongs of others, doesn't revel when others grovel, takes pleasure in the flowering of truth, puts up with anything, trusts God always, always looks for the best, never looks back,
but keeps going to the end.'*

If you replaced the word love in each sentence with your name, would that be how you want to be?

Eg 'Heidi never gives up' or

'Heidi cares more for others than herself etc.'

Idea 4: Imagine this...

Imagine that something negative happens in your life: a parent gets ill, you have only a week to live, a loved one dies. Would it feel important to be cool and popular, look nice, have the best bag or clothes or get only 'A' grades?

If not, what would be important?

Here are some examples of what some young people have said about their values:

'The values that are important to me are loyalty, respect for others, kindness and fun.'

Charlotte, 17

'I would like people to say I am nice to be around, supportive, inspirational and loving.'

Dan, 16

'I would like people to say I am a good person, I am kind and try my best. I would like to be someone who gives good advice and is honest and helpful.'

Leah, 13

'I would like them to say I am funny, energetic, good company and fun to be with, loyal, compassionate, and considerate towards others.'

Dylan, 18

'I would want them to say I was kind and ready to help other people. I would want them to say that I was someone who could get through anything and come out better the other side.'

Abbie, 18

'I want to be healthy and do my best by working hard. I am a Christian and would like people to be able to see that in what I say and do.'

Kaaren, 15

'Trustworthy. Respecting. Loyal. Honest. Good listener. Non judgmental. Down to earth. Helpful. Generous. Supportive. Understanding.'

Laura, 19

'I'd like it if people said I was thoughtful and kind, and that I could be relied on. And that I make people smile:).'

Jess, 19

'I suppose you want to be known for being a good person. Not how smart you are or stuff, but like how you want to be a good person. To be able to do the right thing, even in a wrong situation, is important, and I suppose I'd want people to think that of me. I think, like being true to who you are is important as well.'

Ed, 15

It looks like the most popular values for young people are:

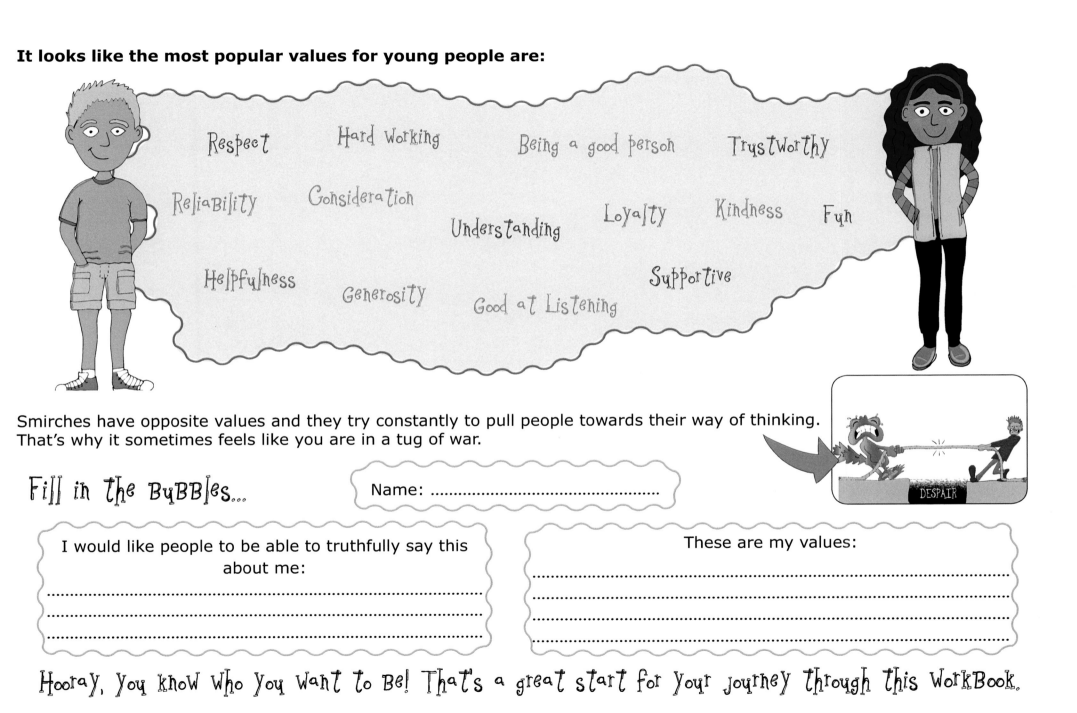

Respect   Hard Working   Being a good person   Trustworthy

Reliability   Consideration   Loyalty   Kindness   Fun

Understanding

Helpfulness   Generosity   Good at Listening   Supportive

Smirches have opposite values and they try constantly to pull people towards their way of thinking. That's why it sometimes feels like you are in a tug of war.

DESPAIR

Fill in the Bubbles...

Name: ....

I would like people to be able to truthfully say this about me:

....
....
....
....

These are my values:

....
....
....
....

Hooray, you know who you want to be! That's a great start for your journey through this workbook.

Smirches love to make you go against your values.

They love it when you are more like them: unkind, impatient, angry, self-absorbed or when you give up. Smirches love it when they trap you into doing the opposite of what you want to do. They play their top songs to make you feel bad until you do something unhealthy or that will upset others. Smirches know that they will win as long as you don't realise their songs are linked to what you do. The smirches think that if they play certain tunes then they can control your actions.

Ask an adult

Do the adults in your life know who they want to be? Ask your parents, teachers and friends about their values - it might help them!

Tune
'You can't do it.'
'Everyone uses you.'

Consequence
You will feel angry and you will shout at your parents

Tune
'You look rubbish.'
'Everyone will stare.'

Consequence
You'll feel scared and won't go to the party.

Tune
'Everyone will leave you.'
'You'll be all alone.'

Consequence
You feel bad and drink lots of alcohol.

Have a drink
Listen to the smirch songs
Harm yourself
Struggle and panic
Shout at your parents
Starve yourself
Do what the crowd says
Deprive yourself of sleep
Smoke

YOUR VALUES

Before you turn the next page

Decide what truly matters to you and what sort of person you want to be. The rest of the workbook will show you how to start noticing what you are doing and how situations, thoughts and feelings change what happens. You will soon be able to see when you are behaving how you want to be and when what you are doing is the opposite of your values: over-indulging in food, cutting yourself, withdrawing or shouting at your family.

Shrinking tip 2
Decide how you are going to get there

Now you know your values you can think about some small steps forward in the right direction. Goals help you to do this.

The smirches want you to share their values, they want you to make shallow goals about the things that don't really matter: losing weight, wearing more make up, buying new things, being popular, getting a boyfriend/girlfriend, earning more money or getting better grades, but what about your values?

Remind yourself of your values from the previous page and then ask yourself three questions:

1. **What am I doing too much that is NOT in line with my values?**

2. **What am I not doing enough that IS in line with my values?**

3. **What do I want to change?**

For your bag

A smart goals page in your journal

SMART goal sheet

Date started: 7th October
Specific Goal To walk to college every day for three weeks
When to achieve by: 28th October

	M	T	W	T	F	S	S
Walk to college every day for three weeks.	✓	✓	✓	✓	✓		
	✓	✓					

Blog Spot

'I realise my smirch now has a face. It is like a little gremlin - short and round, but when it is a better day it has changed to look like Garfield. Sometimes it looks like both!'

Claire

Goals can help you shrink the smirch but only if they are in line with your values.
If one of your values is to try your best, then you might get a good grade, but don't make the grade the goal. If you then get a lower grade you will feel like a failure and the smirch will enjoy being mean to you about it.

You might want to make a goal about eating different stuff. If you are eating the wrong kind of food to comfort yourself when you feel down, choose a goal about feeling more healthy in your mind and body. Make sure it's not about losing weight or looking nicer as that's what the smirch wants.

So you can now think about setting goals to take you in the right direction.

Some sections in this workbook will suggest you set a goal. The mistake people often make is they don't set **SMART** goals and they fail, and then the smirches can quickly discourage them. Make sure any goals you set are:

Specific
Measurable
Adaptive
Realistic
Today

Specific The goal needs to be so clear that anyone reading it could understand and do it, eg 'I will walk to college every Monday'.

Measurable The goal should allow you to measure how well you are doing, eg 'I walked to college every Monday for five weeks'.

Adaptive The goal needs to match your values. Your goal should improve your health or relationships and make the smirch smaller, eg 'More walking will help your mood and make you healthier'.

Realistic Is it reasonable for you? Do you have all you need to succeed? Eg don't join an expensive gym you can't pay for or make the goal so hard that you are likely to fail, like walking to college every day until you leave!

Today Goals Instead of deciding you will make a massive change, eg 'I'll never eat chocolate again', set a 'Today' goal. Decide something you can do for at least a short time, like for a few days or one week. If it works you can do it for longer, eg 'I will drink one less can of fizzy drink'.

Blog Spot

'I have been a bit lazy lately. My smart goal is to load the dishwasher once a week without being asked. My values are to be helpful, kind and have good family relationships.'

Kaaren, 15

Blog Spot

'Deciding on a goal was useful because it gave you something positive to think about and work towards. It provided a sense of achievement even if it was a small goal.'

Katy, 18

Blog Spot

'I am eating too much junk food so I am going to eat two more pieces of fruit per week to improve my health and my concentration.'

Leah, 13

Before you start
Do three things to make your goal smirch proof.

1 Think about all the reasons it won't work.

For example: 'It keeps raining on a Monday', 'I have no decent shoes', 'I will be late for college', 'My brother will say it's pointless'. Think about these problems and solve them before you even start so you will succeed: eg 'I will tell my brother to butt out', 'I will save up for decent shoes and a small coat I can put in my bag'.

2 Focus on the benefits if you obtain this goal

'I will feel less tired, I will be fitter and my mood will improve.' ' I will be proud of myself.'

3 Tell someone about your goal

Smirches prefer secrets so that you only listen to their lyrics.

Each section of this workbook will give you more ideas of things you might like to do in order to shrink your smirch.

Smirch lie

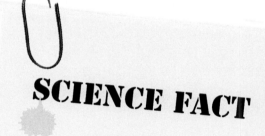

'Goals just make you feel pressured. Leave them on the football field.'

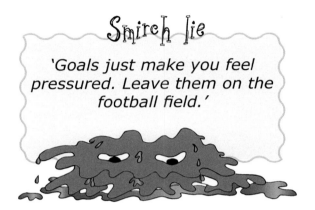

SCIENCE FACT

CONFIDENTIAL
TOP SECRET
CONFIDENTIAL

If you tell others about your goal you will be more likely to succeed.

A colourful journal or notebook

Shrinking tip 3 Be a detective!

Do you watch crime dramas?

Usually they start with the crime, a murder, a burglary or missing person. To solve the crime, the detectives have to find clues: Where did it occur? What happened? Who was there?

The crime is solved when the evidence is gathered and someone puts together all the pieces. Hopefully the criminal can then be captured and locked up.

The smirch is a bit like a criminal, a thief. It likes to be hidden from others and to get on with its bullying in secret. Smirches don't like it when young people start seeing what they actually get up to and where and when they play their best tricks.

To catch and shrink your smirch, you need to start gathering evidence because the more clues you can get about its impact on you, the easier it will be to avoid smirch traps.

All great detectives carry a notebook. To continue your smirch shrinking journey you will need to get hold of a notebook or journal. This will help you collect clues and evidence about what is actually going on in your life so that you get to know when and how to use your smirch shrinking tools.

Shrinking Smog journal

Tues 5th Oct

Feel rubbish. Stayed up all night revising and didn't eat at all. Then got really stressed in my exam and really screwed up. It felt like Smog was sitting on my shoulders making me feel like I was going to fail before I had even started. I'm really stressed coz I know my parents will be really disappointed :(

When you have kept a journal for a few months...

look for the patterns. Smirches thrive when you are unaware of the times when they are strong and you are vulnerable. The more information you have, the more you notice and make sense of their patterns and so the smaller their impact will be on your life.

You will find a way of writing in your journal that works best for you but try and write in it each day at a set time. Lots of young people find just before they go to bed works best.

SPILL all your thoughts, feelings, ideas, worries and things to do into your journal.

PLAN the next day in as much detail as possible. If you don't write down your plan, everything you need to do will spin around in your head driving you crazy and this will stop you enjoying what you are doing.

RECORD anything that might be relevant: food you've eaten, who you are with, places, mood, periods, alcohol, substances, medication, aches and pains. Add five good things from your day.

THINK about what is working well in your life and what you might want to try and do differently.

DECIDE on a today goal for tomorrow!

Smirch lie

'Don't write stuff down. This will make you feel like a right loser.'

Blog Spot

'I enjoyed keeping a journal. I found it useful because I could keep track of my mood which meant I was able to pinpoint more easily the reasons for why I felt how I did at different points throughout the week. I will try to keep it up because it's so nice to be able to reflect on the day, and writing the 5 good things definitely helped me to focus on the better parts and so I ended the day feeling more positive and optimistic.'

Katie, 17

My Journal

Date. 2.12.2016

SPILL: rubbish day, felt really hot and stressy and had a headache, dad being a nightmare, going on and on about me being in my room. He so doesn't understand my life. Katie seemed really off with me today and think she has been talking about me with Kelly as they were together at the weekend. Feel jealous and think I am fat, ugly and boring.

Plan for today

Eat porridge. Check and pack bag: Pack a snack and water

Lessons until 1pm. Eat lunch with Kerry and Abi, (avoid Katie) !!!

2 – 3pm lessons

3.39pm train home Yay!

4pm snack and Tv. 5pm homework

6 –7pm supper with olds. 7pm chill (gadgets away at 9pm)

My today goal: To eat an apple and to avoid Katie Preece (bad influence)

Food and drink: Porridge, kit kat, cheese sandwich, yoghurt, energy drink, lasagne.

Mood weather: Felt anxious this morning but after that a good mood day.

Five things that went well: Didn't see KP, dad said well done, found a fiver in pocket, found maths easy, sunny day.

My smirch played up like this:

When? – when I woke up   Where? – in room   Who was there? – just me   What I did? – had coffee and ciggy

What songs has my smirch been playing? 'Maths will be bad, KP will give me a hard time if don't do as she asks, everyone is brighter and prettier than me.'

What did I do today to try and shrink my smirch? Noticed the songs, avoided KP, took deep breaths in maths.

What else could I try next time? Not having cigarette and coffee when I feel anxious. Try present moment stuff instead (see page 65.)

A journal will...

help you get to know your smirch better and so stop it in its tracks. It will also help you get rid of all the thoughts and feelings that the smirch might have given you. So journals have double shrinking power. In a journal you don't have to fear being judged or need to find the right words.

Chapter 4: Essential Shrinking Tips

The next four shrinking tips are vital shrinking skills to put in your resource bag and should be useful to everyone. These are:

- Notice **(N)**
- Breathe **(B)**
- Present Moment **(P)**
- Stop **(S)**

The first letter of each word make **NBPS** so perhaps that could stand for a personal message to your smirch.

No Bullying PATHETIC smirch!

SCIENCE FACT

Did you know humans have three brains in one? Right in the middle of the human brain is a brain like a lizard, around that is a brain like a dog and covering up these two brains is brain three, the cerebral cortex. Only humans have brain three and this gives us the ability to talk, think, plan and have faith. When we are stressed the cerebral cortex gets a bit sleepy and the lizard brain takes over. Think of a lizard – pretty much all they can do is hiss, bite and run away. These next four essential shrinking tips are to help you spend more of your time in human brain mode and less time in lizard brain, as lizards can't notice or follow their chosen values.

Shrinking tip 4 Notice

For your bag

A cheerful pen to jot down things you notice and observe about yourself and what happens in your life.

The smirches find it strange...

that most young people understand very complex gadgets but they don't know much about their own minds. Observing what you think and feel at different times and in different situations is the first step to feeling better and getting closer to the values you have chosen that are important to you.

Learning to notice or observe what you are thinking, feeling and doing, and why, is a skill that you can learn and has **MASSIVE** smirch shrinking power.

'My days are very similar - I have the same emotions at similar times every day. I think too much. Writing down a list of things I feel and worry about made it easier to think of ways to overcome them.'

Katy, 18

Blog Spot

What is there to notice?

Have a look out of the window. Can you observe and describe what the weather is like at this minute? Is it cloudy, raining, wet, dark, sunny or calm. Moods are a bit like the weather inside of you. When you are feeling happy, it is sunny, when you are grumpy or sad, it is dark and cloudy, and when you are angry perhaps it is like a head and body storm.

THINK: What is the weather like in your mind and body right now?

Now, take a few minutes to sit quietly and notice your breathing. Notice how fast or slow your breathing is, then have a look around you and observe what you can see. Notice five things and then listen carefully to what you can hear. If you can do this, you have discovered that there are two parts to your mind (not many people know that!).

Part 1: the part of you that is breathing, seeing and hearing

Part 2: the part of you that is observing or noticing the breathing, seeing and hearing.

Can you also observe your thoughts?

What are you thinking right now? Perhaps thoughts about this book, 'it's stupid, I don't like it', or thoughts about what happened today, 'I can't believe I said that!', 'the teacher kept staring at me', or worries about tomorrow, 'will that friend talk to me?', 'will my hair look ok?', 'are my parents going to argue?'

Remember the smirch is a mind bully, it has no power outside of the mind. All the smirch wants to do is hook you back in your mind to keep you thinking about what is going on in your head and stop you enjoying life. Like most bullies the smirch likes to stay invisible, not get spotted or noticed. So once you start noticing the changes in your mind weather, the smirch starts shrinking straight away.

You might notice when you hang out with a certain group that you feel anxious. Going out to parties or speaking in class might result in your stomach churning. Perhaps the smirchipod gets turned up when you know a certain lesson is coming up or you have to spend time with a relative you don't like. Start to notice the patterns and write them in your journal.

Can you also start to notice when you feel good, calm and happy?

Sitting at your gran's watching TV with a piece of cake?

In the car with your dad?

Playing football or riding your bike?

Listening to music?

Talking to a friend you trust?

Ask an adult

Ask other people you trust these questions about what they notice.

When am I most relaxed and sunny?

When do I seem most stressy?

What situations and people take me away from who I want to be?

Can you start to see...

that the lyrics the smirch plays in your head as thoughts can change how your body feels and how you feel emotionally? Can you start to notice what you do in certain situations when you feel anxious, when you feel down, when someone upsets or angers you? Can you start to recognise when the smirch has hooked you back in your head with a thought, a scary picture or a bad memory? If you can notice throughout the day when you are really enjoying what is going on rather than being entangled in your head, this will be a massive step forward.

There will be much more about noticing as we get shrinking. Remember to write anything you observe in your journal. The more clues you can collect, the quicker this smirch will start to feel smaller.

Practice Ideas

Set an alarm on your mobile to prompt you to stop at least three times a day to observe:

- The most frequent lyrics your smirch plays (thoughts) and in what situations they start playing.

- How your body feels physically and how you feel emotionally.

- What weather mood are you in?

Choose one day and pretend that the person who writes the best description of exactly what happened in their day will win a million pounds. Describe in your journal as much detail as you can about what you did and how you felt in every different room and situation. Describe the comments that made you feel OK and the ones that upset you. Describe the times you felt calm and the times you felt worried, stressed or angry. Describe the impact each person you met had on you, the ones that made you feel better, the ones that made you feel good and the ones that made you feel tense or fearful.

Smirch lie

'Don't watch, we will only frighten you.'

Shrinking tip 5 Breathe with Your Belly

For your bag

Pictures of lungs in different places to rem you to Belly Breathe

You might think Breathing is easy...

but many people are breathing badly, which is making them feel stressed. You might actually be taking short, shallow breaths, a bit like a dog panting. (Remember, we should not aim to be like our pets!) Smirches know that shallow breathing causes a lack of fresh air; this is good for them as they know shallow breathing easily becomes a habit and keeps people feeling stressed. In order to feel calm you need to give your body and brain enough oxygen by 'belly breathing'.

Imagine a situation...

where you feel very relaxed: sitting by a swimming pool, listening to nice music or watching a great DVD with your feet up on the settee. When you are relaxed, you will be taking around seven breaths a minute, and to do this you have to be breathing slowly and deeply. One name for this sort of breathing is belly breathing (the posh term is diaphragmatic breathing). Belly breathing tricks the smirch and your body into thinking you are calm even when you are not.

Belly Breathing...

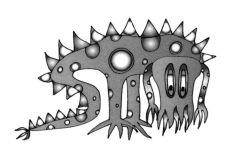

makes the smirches run and hide; they find it exhausting to watch! It will help you if you can improve your breathing at all times, but it will especially help when you feel stressed or frightened or when you need to focus to do something like an exam or an interview.

Blog Spot

'I practised from a video; I did it at home after school in my bedroom. It didn't take very long to learn. I felt calmer and more relaxed after doing it.'

Tom, 13

How to Belly Breathe
Katy, 18

- **Make** sure you are lying down, standing or sitting upright.

- **Place** a hand on your tummy - this helps you tell whether or not you are breathing deeply.

- **Breathe** in slowly through your mouth. Keep breathing in past the point you would normally stop. Imagine you are blowing up a balloon inside you and you want it to be really big. (Count to 6)

- **When** your lungs are fully inflated you can feel your diaphragm being pushed down inside you.

- **Hold** the air in your lungs for a couple of seconds before breathing out slowly through your nose. (Count to 8)

Blog Spot

'I have had some panic problems over the last week. I told my mum and we started to look at websites on breathing techniques. It really helped to breathe and I really enjoyed learning and watching the videos. Now I have to remember to use it when I feel in a panic. So I have written down some ideas in my school rough book so I can use them when I need to.'

Matthew, 13

Blog Spot

'When you are breathing well, put a hand on your stomach which should move out when you breathe in. Your hand on your chest shouldn't move too much.'

Johanna, 16

Blog Spot

'I had been taught belly breathing before but I needed to practise it a few times to start feeling the benefits. I found it helpful to remember it's like your abdomen is a balloon - when you breathe out your balloon shrinks because all the air has been let out. I mostly practised at night before going to bed. It does really help.'

Katie, 17

Practice ideas

If you put deep breathing into your search engine there are loads of helpful videos. Choose which one you like and practise with and without the video. There are some good apps too.

To learn any new skill...

the brain needs lots of practice until it becomes automatic and the old habits disappear. Few people can get on a bike, learn the piano or a new language in a few hours. Belly breathing is the same: you have to practise.

If you can do this for just five minutes twice a day, you will notice a reduction in anxiety and feelings of stress within a couple of weeks.

Smirch lie

'Belly breathing makes you fat.'

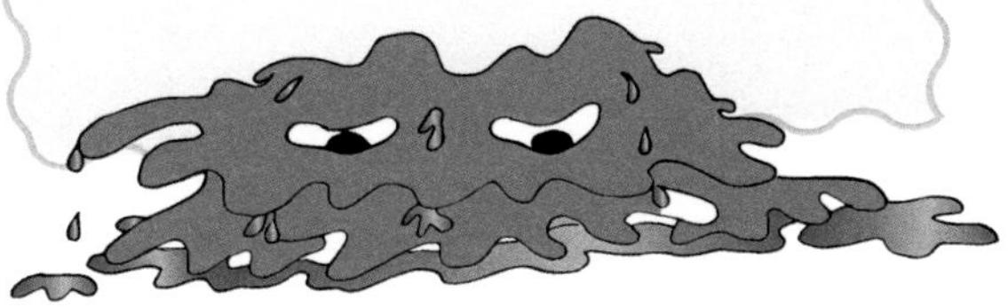

Blog Spot

'I found a YouTube video by GoZen with the 4-7-8 breathing exercise really helpful to learn belly breathing. It took something quite serious and simplified it and made it funny and engaging. It took me about 30 seconds to learn. I practised it a couple of times a day on the train to and from school.'

Katy, 18

Breathing with your Belly...

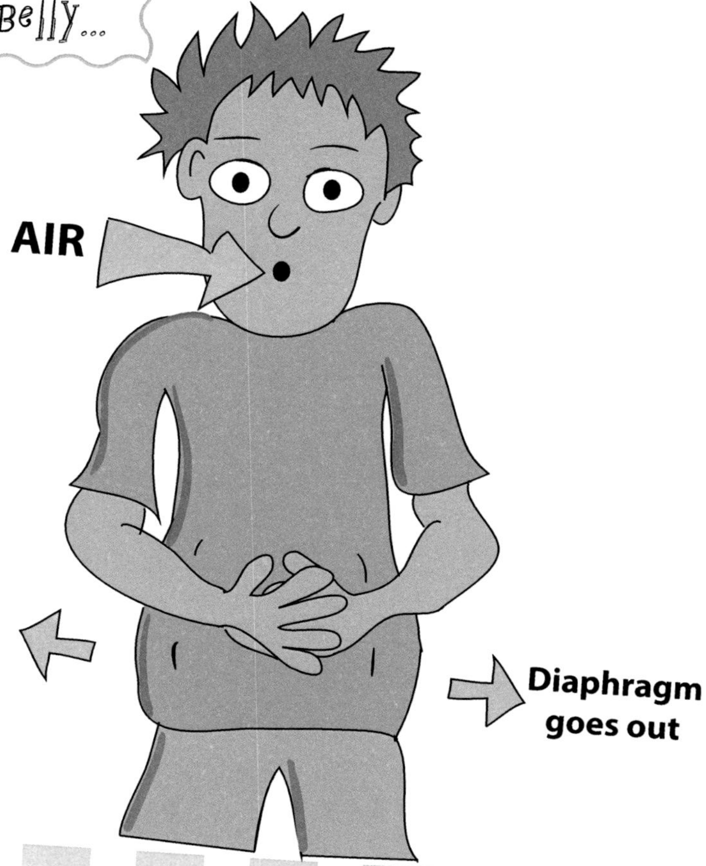

AIR

Diaphragm goes out

Practice ideas

Take time throughout your day to notice your breathing and, if it is fast and shallow, take a few minutes to do ten belly breaths.

Shrinking tip 6 Get present

You need to get Present

No! not get **a present**, get **present**. Being Present is the opposite of being on autopilot or having your head in the clouds, really noticing what you can see, smell, hear and touch around you at this moment. The smirch knows that the way to feel calm is to pay attention to where you are and what you are doing.

Some people call this mindfulness

Instead of having your mind full of all the things going on in your head, you are aware of what is happening around you. Learning to be present is actually SO simple but also SO hard. The more you start to notice whether or not you are connected to the real world, you will see how easy it is for the smirch to hook you back into your thoughts with a worrying lyric or picture.

Our five senses

Our five senses allow us to enjoy: food, the sound of music, the beauty of a sunny day, the smell of doughnuts, the feel of a hug or our feet in the sea—our lives! In order to really enjoy the life we have we need to pay attention to what we can see, hear, touch, smell and taste whatever we are doing.

 Seeing

 Hearing

 Tasting

 Smelling

 Touching

If you are not doing one of these five things, you are not paying attention and you are probably caught up in your thinking, listening to smirch tunes about: 1. The past: *I wish I hadn't shouted at my dad at home.*
2. The future: *Will Katie Preece be nasty or nice today in the sixth form area?*
3. What others are thinking: *He looked at me, everyone hates my new haircut.*

The smirch knows...

that if people start getting present, their relationships get better and their minds and bodies get healthier. They know that when you are on autopilot you:

- Don't enjoy what is happening in front of you.

- Don't listen or learn.

- Feel stressed, upset and anxious about your thoughts.

- Get angry or upset with the wrong people.

Practice ideas

Choose a 'get present' reminder. Choose something you wear or have with you most of the time as your reminder (eg a piece of jewellery, a watch, an item of clothing or a zip or button on your bag).

Every time you see this reminder, take a couple of minutes to be aware of the present moment using your senses. Choose one of the five sense exercises to use each time or if you have time, do all five (see page 68).

(see page 68).

'My parents took me to a lovely restaurant for my birthday. I was worrying about people finding out I was here and saying I am posh. I didn't even taste the food. My mum said I was really grumpy and it was a waste of money. I felt upset I had ruined everything again.'

Kylie, 16

Blog Spot

SCIENCE FACT

Practising being in the present moment, paying attention on purpose, has been shown to calm the activity in the parts of the brain that make you angry, stressed and anxious (lizard and dog brain).

If you can learn to be present, you will have discovered something that will help you for the rest of your life.

The smirches hate people getting present as all of their power slips away.

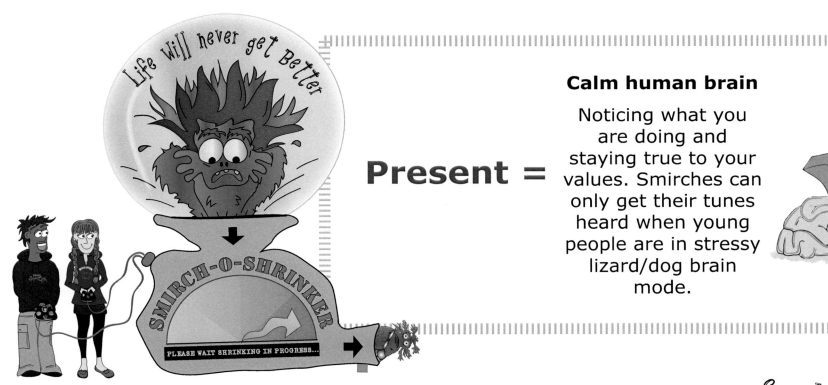

Life will never get better

SMIRCH-O-SHRINKER

PLEASE WAIT SHRINKING IN PROGRESS...

Present =

Calm human brain

Noticing what you are doing and staying true to your values. Smirches can only get their tunes heard when young people are in stressy lizard/dog brain mode.

Blog Spot

'I was watching a film with some mates but all I could think of was I am the only one with a rubbish T-shirt on.'

Mark, 15

Smirch lie

'Keep daydreaming, it's better than real life.'

Sight

Take a few belly breaths and look and see where you are. What can you see now you are looking that you hadn't been aware of. Count five things you can see. Choose one object to study in detail as if you have never seen it before. Notice the colours, the shape, the shadows on the object and around it. Take a few more breaths and then bring your attention back to what you are doing.

The five senses exercises

Practise using your five senses as much as you can and you will get better at noticing. These quick techniques take just a few minutes to do and you can also use them if you are feeling impatient in a queue or waiting for a lift or about to sit an exam.

Smell

Take a few belly breaths and become aware of what you can smell. Does this room smell different to others, is it nice, does it remind you of anything? Turn your head and see if you can smell anything else, smell any objects near to you or your clothes (if no one is looking!). Really breathe in and notice the smells. Take a few more breaths and then bring your attention back to what you are doing.

Taste

Take a few deep breaths. Notice whether your mouth has any obvious taste, lick your lips and see if you can taste anything different, swallow and see if this changes the taste in your mouth. Is what you can taste nice or not? If you have something to eat, take a mouthful and really notice what it tastes like as if you have never eaten this food before. Take a few more breaths and then bring your attention back to what you are doing.

Touch

Choose an object in front of you and touch it: A book, a pen, a picture frame or material. Take a few deep belly breaths. If you are on your own, close your eyes. Feel the object as if you have never touched it before or as if you can't see, feel the curves, see how the different parts feel different to each other, notice if it's hot or cold, notice if smooth or rough. Notice your clothes and observe which bits of clothing you can feel without moving and what they feel like. Take a few more breaths and then bring your attention back to what you are doing.

Hearing

Stop for a minute and become aware of the sounds you can hear: talking, the clock ticking, birds screeching or singing, cars, your own breathing. See how many sounds you can identify in just this place. See if you can hear more and more things each time you do it. Take a few more breaths and then bring your attention back to what you are doing.

Shrinking tip 7 STOP

Put together noticing, breathing **and** get present.

You have now learnt three essential smirch shrinking tips: **Noticing** what is going on, **belly breathing** and **getting present**. The smirch is shuddering as it knows it's time for you to bring them all together and that the clear message is **N**o **B**ullying **P**athetic **S**mirch. Can you see it shrinking? Is the power balance changing?

STOP is a technique to use to make you feel more stable when you feel emotionally overwhelmed. Maybe you feel:

You just want to scream

Stressed out of your human Brain

Confused, upset or frightened

Lost for words

So low you want to Binge, cut, drink or smoke

Close to a panic attack

For your bag

Red stickers to remind you to STOP

The smirch is shouting its nasty tunes at you:
'Look at the state of you!'
'You will fail, you wimp!'
'Everyone is staring!'
'Loser, loser, loser!'

THE STOP TECHNIQUE

Stop and get present, just stand or sit still, what can you see, hear and smell?
Remind yourself of what someone you love would say.

Take some deep belly breaths and push your feet down on the floor and straighten your back.

Observe what is going on? What am I thinking and feeling? What are the words that my smirch is saying? What physical sensations do I notice in my body?

Press on and ask yourself. 'What can I do that will be best for me and others and that will keep me close to my values?' Do it despite your feelings.

Practice ideas

Think through some recent situations when you have felt stressed or overwhelmed.

Imagine yourself stopping and practising the STOP technique.

Ask an adult

What would someone who loves you say when you feel overwhelmed, panicky and upset?

Write it down so you can learn it for when you get upset.

Whenever you see a red traffic light or STOP sign...

practise the STOP technique. Buy some red stickers or ones with the word STOP on and put them in different places - your school book, your phone, your bag or desk at home - to remind you to practise STOP.

Chapter 5: Thinking and Feeling

Smirches are very good at playing you thoughts that tempt you to tune in.

The smirches know that if you don't notice what you are doing you are an easy target and more likely to upset people and do things that will make you unhealthy.

This chapter will help you become more aware of the thinking, feeling, doing cycle and give you some ideas of ways to cope with any difficult thoughts and feelings.

Shrinking tip 8 Take the Bag off your head

For your bag

My favourite ideas to manage difficult thoughts (see Page 75–76)

Sometimes people say the following rhyme to children:

'Sticks and stones will break my bones but names will never hurt me!' Your smirch knows this is so **NOT** true. The smirch knows that physical pain is often easier to bear than people calling you spiteful names. The smirch knows words are very powerful.

Three important facts you need to know about thoughts (smirch lyrics)

1

Thoughts are powerful and can change how you are feeling and what you do

Stop for a minute and remember the last time you felt really embarrassed. Close your eyes and remember as much detail as you can: Who was there? What did you say or do? How did you feel?

How does this make you feel?

Ashamed, embarrassed or anxious? Sick in your stomach? Heart pounding? Sweating? Red in the face?

Now close your eyes and think about a lemon. Imagine cutting it in half and sucking out all the juice. What happened in your mouth? What have you just done? Of course, there are no lemons and you have not just embarrassed yourself. BUT you have used thoughts to make you feel the same emotions and physical sensations that you would feel if you were actually embarrassed or sucking a lemon!

WOW, the thoughts and words in your head are very powerful!

I am a rubbish friend.

Why me?

If only I had a better...

I am not as good as others.

It's just not fair.

Thoughts can stop us enjoying life

When we are awake, a lot of the time we are listening and reacting to thoughts and memories in our head. These thoughts are just random words but they have the power to make us feel happy, sad, upset and angry (remember the lemon). The smirch would like to throw sticks and stones but it has no arms and legs. Thoughts are its best weapon as it can only bully you in your head.

Put a large cloth, sports or paper bag over your head
(not a plastic one!)

Pull the bag down to your shoulders.
Now try to do the following things with the bag on your head: watch something on TV, read a page of this book, text a friend.

If you haven't got a bag, imagine how your day would have been if you had done everything with a thick bag on your head.

You are probably thinking this is a stupid idea as no one would wear a bag on their head BUT this is how life is when you are focusing only on your thoughts and smirch songs. You are missing your life and you might as well have a bag on your head! It is a bit like listening all day to a sad television or radio programme in your mind.

Can you see how spending lots of time listening to a bad TV programme could stop you enjoying life? You certainly can't be in the present moment.

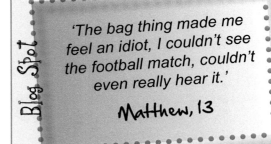

'I put a large handbag on my head, I couldn't see or hear anything.'

Kaaren, 15

Blog Spot

Blog Spot

'The bag thing made me feel an idiot, I couldn't see the football match, couldn't even really hear it.'

Matthew, 13

Thoughts are often not true

Try this: Say in your mind, 'my arm is paralysed' and at the same time scratch your ear. Now say, 'I am turning blue.'

Check the mirror to see whether the thoughts are true or not. Are you turning blue? Is your arm paralysed?

When we have thoughts like: 'you are rubbish' or 'you will fail' or 'everyone hates you' we feel upset because we react as if these things are true. But remember, thoughts are only words in your head. It is normal to have thoughts that are random, untrue and even a little mad! You don't have to believe your thoughts.

Here are some typical examples of unhelpful thought patterns.

Get into detective mode and notice when you fall into these thinking traps.

Believing your feelings

'I feel scared so I must be in danger.' 'I feel embarrassed so I am an idiot.'

Negative labels

Using negative labels for yourself or others in response to small mistakes: 'I'm so stupid.' 'He is such a loser.'

Mind reading

Thinking you can read other people's minds. 'He looked at me strangely because I am ugly.'

All or nothing

Thinking: 'If I don't get 100% I have failed.' 'I made a small mistake so there is no point in trying.'

Taking the blame

When a situation goes wrong, you take the blame even if it wasn't anything to do with you.

Making things seem bigger

Blowing things out of proportion: 'I got a lower grade than usual so I am going to fail my exams, get thrown out of school and be unemployed.'

You need to add to your resource bag ways of taking the bag off your head or ignoring what is on the radio programme. So you can get present, enjoy your life and feel calmer.

Here are my five favourite ideas to take the bag off your head and make your thoughts feel less scary and powerful.

Idea 1. Noticing when you are on auto-pilot

Start to notice when you have the bag on your head, when you are not paying attention to what is happening.

1. Look out for signs you are on auto-pilot. Perhaps you drop something or walk the wrong way, or you suddenly realise you don't know what your friend or teacher is saying. These are signs you are locked into your head and listening to the smirch.

2. Start to notice throughout the day. Are you in the present moment or in your head listening to thoughts, memories and worries? If you are in your head, what lyrics are playing? We all have our favourites. Maybe yours are: 'everyone hates me', 'I am not popular', 'all the teachers hate me', 'what will it be like at home?', 'I will fail'.

3. Can you label the type of thinking you are doing? Is it planning? worrying? fearing? daydreaming? boiling in anger? resenting? Say to yourself: 'The smirch tune has got me worrying'. Then see if you can name the song. You will have a favourite few that appear time and time again: 'My rubbish clothes', 'Why am I treated like this?', 'The difficult friend ', 'The failed exams ', 'My dysfunctional family'.

4. Sometimes it will be enough to just notice and label your thoughts. Other times, you will need to try the other four ideas in this section in order to ignore the smirch songs. Remember that these are just words and pictures in your head and everyone has them, but mostly they are not helpful or truthful.

Idea 2. Weird But helpful

Get a piece of card. Write down all the nasty things your smirch says when it really wants to upset or scare you. 'I am stupid', 'no one likes me', 'what are they thinking?', 'you're a loser', 'you are ugly', 'you are fat', 'you are too thin and small', 'your family is rubbish', 'your Dad doesn't love you', 'you are not wanted', 'something bad will happen.'

If all these thoughts were part of a book about your life, what would the title be? Maybe: *You Are Not Good Enough* or *Mad Family* or maybe *The Fat and Ugly Girl* or *The Messed-up Thin Boy.* Write the title on the back of the card. Words and smirch lyrics have more power in your head and when you try not to listen. The more you read them, the less power they will have when they pop in your head. When one of the thoughts pops into your head, you can say 'oh yes' this is the mad family story or the tale of the fat and ugly girl. Hide the card but read the thoughts as much as you can. At first they will make you feel bad but take some belly breaths and keep reading them as many times a day as you can until they don't have a big impact on you.

Idea 3. Make it less personal

When you notice a negative or scary thought, add to the beginning: **'I am having the thought that...'** So for example: **'I am having the thought that...** I am stupid at school'. **'I am having the thought that...** everyone hates me.' **'I am having the thought that...** my parents will die.'

This makes it feel a bit less personal and reminds you that thoughts are not facts, they are words in your head, sometimes true, sometimes rubbish and sometimes really odd.

Idea 4. Get the opinion of a sensible group of people

Work out what thought has upset you.

'I am a bad daughter', 'I am rubbish at school', 'I am stupid', 'I will fail', 'I am getting worse', 'it is the beginning of a bad week'.

Imagine a panel of sensible, truthful people who have to decide if this thought is the truth. Would they have any evidence against you? What is the evidence for and against?

Am I stupid?

'I am good at lots of things but find maths hard', 'People tell me my ideas are good','I have just been put up a set in science', 'I have just made one mistake'.

The verdict: I am not stupid.

'I am a bad child and now something bad will happen.' 'I forgot my homework and then shouted at my mum.'

Am I a horrible person?

'Everyone shouts sometimes.' 'She knows I love her.' 'I spend lots of time helping her most weekends.' 'I was disorganised and I over-reacted.' 'I apologised and gave her a hug.'

The verdict: I am an OK child and shouting won't cause my mum to have an accident.

Idea 5. Ask Yourself: Is this helpful?

When you realise your thinking is in overdrive and you are feeling panicky, work out what you are thinking. It may be 'I will fail all my exams' or 'I have too much to do' or maybe 'I have a rubbish life'.

Notice how these thoughts make you feel. Notice what you are feeling tempted to do: maybe binge on fast food, smoke weed, go to bed or self harm. Ask yourself: 'Are these thoughts helping me?', 'Are they helping me get closer to my values?' and 'Do they make me feel better?' If not, try the other ideas in this chapter, take the bag off your head and ignore the smirch songs!

SCIENCE FACT

Every day we have about 50,000 thoughts. Most of them won't be kind, helpful or true!

You have allowed your smirch to bully you for ages so it will take practice to learn to use these ideas so they work.

Smirch lie

All your thoughts are true.

So..

you just need to start noticing when the smirch pulls you into your head. As you practise you will get quicker at coming back into the present moment and feel mentally much better for it. The smirch knows that the easiest way to keep you feeling stressed is to make you spend as much time as possible listening to their tunes and watching their movies.

When you have noticed you have been pulled into your head, you can picture yourself taking off the bag, taking out the ear plugs and parachuting back into your life. Pretend you are someone arriving from a new planet. What can you see? Notice the colours and shapes of the things around. What are you actually doing? What are you watching? What should you be paying attention to?

Ask an adult

Ask other people what their popular smirch tunes are.

Blog Spot

'I realised one of the bad things I do is look at what everyone else is doing on my phone when I get home from college. My smirch then says, "you are boring, no-one likes you, you are not as good as her". It has been so hard but I have stopped looking at my phone until my sister gets in as when you are looking at my phone until my sister gets in as when you are with someone the smirch isn't so shouty.'

Kaaren, 15

Blog Spot

'In physics yesterday I remembered the rows my parents are having. The teacher shouted at me as I couldn't answer a simple question. I wasn't listening. I was quite pleased though as I noticed what had happened for the first time, the smirch had played me thoughts like "your parents will split", "your life will be rubbish". I listened and didn't pay attention, then when I got shouted at the smirch played "you are a thick loser". I wrote it in my journal last night. It was actually a eureka moment.'

Luke, 18

Blog Spot

'I saw how I am always in my head. When I talk to my mates I don't listen, I think, what do they think of me, I am so uncool, everyone likes him better. I realised I look a bit stupid sometimes as I am so in my head that I am not in the group chat at all. I am trying really hard to get present and listen to what people are saying. It's actually great, if you stop thinking about yourself, you feel better.'

Ryan, 15

Shrinking tip 9 Feel the fear

For your bag

a 'calm Box'

Your smirch wants you to Believe...

that no one else has bad feelings like insecurity, sadness, anger or anxiety and everybody else you know is happy all the time. They try to hide the fact that **ALL** experiences and relationships produce negative **and** positive feelings.

So the only way to keep free of negative feelings would be to have no contact with other humans or even pets. However, that probably won't make you feel happy either. Think of any good relationship or activity that you enjoy. This could be a pet, a parent, your closest friend, a new school, an interesting subject or simply watching a film. These all give many benefits.

But with every relationship and activity there also come negative feelings like

Guilt	Anxiety	Fear	Distress	Sadness	Disappointment
'I have not seen my close friend much.' *'I could be a better son.'*	*'Will I pass my exam in my best subject?'* *'Is this the right college?'*	*'I will fail my exams.'* *'Will my parents split up?'* *'My group might reject me'*	*'My friend has cancer.'* *'I have too much homework.'*	*'I miss my Mum.'* *'My cat died.'* *'I miss my old school.'*	*'My grade wasn't good.'* *'My Dad is in trouble.'* *'My brother was late.'*

All experiences and relationships make you feel all of the normal human emotions at some point, negative and positive. Even when life is feeling pretty good sometimes you will feel sad, angry, upset or worried. That is what life is like.

Your smirch is mean so it likes to remind you of what your parents and teachers told you as a younger child: 'it's not that bad', 'don't make a fuss', 'put on a brave face' and 'boys don't cry'.

Smirches want you to believe that you can stop your bad feelings when they know humans can't. When you feel bad they want you to believe you have these negative feelings because you are weak, stupid or a failure in comparison to all the other young people around you, who certainly are not experiencing any.

your feelings can be compared to the weather: storms, sunshine and rain. Feelings are as changeable as the weather. How much would you get done if you only went out when it was sunny? Your smirch wants you to be like that in response to your feelings. It wants you to stay in if you feel bad and only do things when you feel sunny and confident. They know then you won't get much done.

The smirch knows young people hate feeling bad and will often miss out on things to avoid the risk of feeling anxious, embarrassed or sad. Can you notice how a bad feeling or even the fear of one makes you lose out?

Thought or feeling
Outcome

'If I go to the party, people might look at me, I will have a panic attack.'
Don't go to the party

'I will miss the cinema trip as it will make me anxious.'
Don't see friends

'If I audition for a part in the play, I might get rejected.'
Don't apply

'I am too fed up to go out.'
Stay in on your own

'If I go to the sleepover, I might get homesick or scared.
Miss out on fun

'I will only get a job when I feel confident enough.'
Have no money

The smirches are jumping with joy!

They are just delighted! They have made a normal feeling like anxiety or sadness feel massive. Then you cancel your friend or take a day off school and shout at your parents whilst looking at Facebook to see how everyone else is out having fun. Your smirch then reminds you that you have failed again and plays a song to make you feel worse like, 'you are such an epic failure', 'loser loser loser'.

Bad feelings are normal but humans don't like them. Often it is not the bad feelings that cause your distress but your struggle to be free of them, or what you do to try and get rid of them.

So what can you do?

Notice

You should be getting to understand the concept of noticing now. You are becoming more aware of your thoughts, your ups and downs. Now start to notice your feelings, the physical sensations in your body, your emotions.

Name that feeling

When you wake up, when you are doing different things, when you try to sleep, just notice what feelings come up, and try and decide what emotion it is. Is it anxiety? Is it anger? Is it excitement? Is it low mood? See if you can notice when different emotions come. By noting in your journal you will start to see patterns. When does your smirch make you feel anxious? What were you doing? Try and see if you can notice what tunes or images the smirch has been playing or what situation you are in.

The smirch will not be happy if the 'thinking, feeling, doing' loop becomes clearer to you. It knows that will give you a massive surge of strength.

Nobody likes negative feelings. Most people do one of three things when they start to feel Bad:

1. Get anxious or stressed about having the feeling, get really tense, breathe too quickly and feel worse. This is like turning on a struggle switch, it makes the bad feeling get much worse.

2. Try and get rid of it by doing something. You probably have a favourite thing: exercising, going to bed, hurting yourself, shouting at others, playing loud music, bingeing on food or drink, avoiding or running away from the situation.

3. Try and ignore it. The smirch makes this option impossible as they will make sure the feeling grabs your attention with a good lyric like, 'here it comes again', 'this is so horrid', or 'you won't cope'.

If bad feelings are **normal** and you can't get rid of them, the only way to stop yourself feeling like you have been pulled into the pit of despair is to learn ways to experience bad feelings but not get overwhelmed by them.

Here are a few of my favourite techniques for managing Bad feelings:

1. Pretend you are a scientist investigating a new phenomenon...

- **When** you feel a bad feeling, take a few belly breaths and try and relax your body.
- **Pretend** you are feeling something new for the first time. Show interest.
- **Focus** on your body. Start at your head and work down.
- **Notice** where in your body the feeling is strongest.
- **What** does it feel like? Where does it start and stop? Is it moving? Is it hot or cold?
- **Name** the emotion; say, 'this is fear'.
- **Continue** to observe.
- **Breathe** slowly and deeply.
- **Imagine** your breath flowing into your emotion: it's as if you are giving it space, not trying to push it out.
- **Notice** your body, notice your breath. You don't have to like it.
- **Notice** what the rest of your body feels like, what else you can see and hear.
- **Try** and do this until you feel that you can get on with what you need to do.

2. Bad feelings are sometimes a bit like a smoke alarm

They alert us there is a problem. Often that problem is caused by what tunes and films are being played in our heads. Can you notice what you have been thinking or worrying about to cause this feeling? If so, practise some of the techniques you already know to help with your thoughts and do some belly breathing and quick present moment techniques.

Blog Spot
'Weird I know but popping bubble wrap really helps me calm down when I feel angry or upset.'
Lee, 17

3. Allocate the smirch a strict time to visit...

(perhaps five minutes in the morning and evening, but not too near your bedtime). Give yourself this time to worry and think about your smirch, what it has made you think, feel and do. Write down your worries and what you are afraid of. Some fears might be real, some not, but whatever they are they will be much less scary on paper. 'I am afraid of dying, getting fat, losing my mind, being in a wheelchair, crying in public, failing, never getting a job.' Fears are much less useful to the smirch in black and white than when they are running as tunes in your head. Then practise some belly breaths and connect back to the present.

4. A box in your bag

When you are really upset it can be hard to know what might help. This can sometimes make you do things that help in that moment but are not good for you in the long term. It can be useful to keep a calm bag or box so that when you feel overwhelmingly distressed you can go to your bag or box and find something that will help. When you are feeling calm, collect together items that you know help when you feel upset. Include things that you can see, eat, feel and touch.

5. Do an activity that absorbs you

Think of a positive mental or physical activity to do despite your bad feelings, eg puzzle books, electronic games, make a picture or card, bake a cake, go for a walk etc. Write a list of your ideas and keep it in your journal or calm bag as sometimes it is hard to think when you are experiencing lots of bad feelings.

6. Remember this feeling shows
you are a normal human being who has a heart and cares. If you didn't have bad feelings, you wouldn't have good ones either and then you would be a robot.

'When I feel the smirch has pulled me into the pit, I notice and I get out my calm box. It has my best funny DVD, photos of friends and family, some nice perfume and the card my gran sent me. It reminds me she loved me and wanted me to be OK.'

Kylie, 15

Practice ideas

When you feel calm, get a large ice cube and sit and hold it until it starts to hurt. This is similar to when you experience emotional pain. Practise the curious scientist idea on page 81, really notice where is the pain, what does it feel like?

Notice what your smirch is telling you: You won't cope, this hurts too much, panic, drop it. See if you can observe those tricky thoughts but ignore them. Take some good belly breaths, relax your shoulders and get present by noticing what's coming to each of your senses (see shrinking tip 6).

Notice how the pain is easier to bear when you relax. Notice that when you forget and tense up, it is like you have turned on the struggle switch and the pain feels more severe.

Practise this many times until you can manage physical pain using your favourite smirch shrinking techniques. You can then use the same strategies when you feel sad, upset or angry.

Practice ideas

Jump up and down until you feel hot and out of breath. Notice what your body feels like. You will probably be sweating, heart racing, red in the face and panting like a dog. This is due to a large surge of adrenalin. This is the same body response you get when you experience a bad feeling like fear, panic or anxiety. The reason you probably don't feel anxious is because you are too out of breath to listen to smirch lyrics.

Now sit down and prove to yourself you can get yourself out of this state. Slow your breathing with deep belly breaths, push your feet down on the floor and notice what that feels like and then get into the present moment. Notice how long it takes for your body to feel calm. Next time you are feeling panicky, remind yourself that it will take a few minutes to calm your body but that you can do it. Practise this until you feel confident you can calm your body when you need.

Watch a YouTube video of a wave with a bird on the top! Watch how the bird stays on top even though the wave goes really high and low. This is what our emotions are like – fear, anxiety, sadness – they come in waves, you can't get rid of them but you can learn to surf.

The key To coping with negative feelings...

is learning not to tense up and panic in response to emotional pain. You can practise this when you experience mild physical pain like when you stub your toe or feel too hot or cold. Take some belly breaths, relax your body and try and notice what the pain is actually like instead of getting tense and putting on the struggle switch.

Write a letter to yourself and put it in your calm box or somewhere safe, write to yourself as if you were a friend feeling low or anxious. Tell yourself you have coped with this before, remind yourself what helps and that it will soon get better.

Smirch lie

'Bad feelings will control and even kill you.'

Shrinking tip 10 Get more present

Quick Present moment techniques...

should already be in your smirch shrinking bag but this section includes more present moment strategies. These are so important for mind fitness and will help you manage all those tricky thoughts and feelings you are now noticing. Remember it's just about paying attention on purpose through your five senses.

The smirch hates it. Your smirch wants you to think about the past or worry about the future but it knows when you start paying attention you can only think about the **NOW**. Start by noticing your next three breaths, stop reading and just pay attention to your breathing. **Hooray! You are in the NOW.**

Every time you have a thought...

brain cells (neurons) connect like little impulses across your brain. When these brain cells connect, your brain grows thicker and stronger in certain places based on the thoughts you think. You can actually change the wiring of the brain to help you be calmer by just choosing to think in a certain way. Just like a bodybuilder lifting weights to build muscle, the more time you spend in the present moment, the stronger the part of your brain that allows you to experience calm feelings will become.

Imagine that the 'get present' noticing part of your brain is

a muscle in your head. At the moment it's flabby and can't do what it is supposed to. You need to practise paying attention and getting present until that muscle is toned. If you go to the gym on just one day for ten minutes you won't get toned muscles; you have to go lots of times over many months or they will get flabby again. It's the same, practising getting present, really noticing what is happening takes time and practice.

For your bag

An 'adults' book of colouring patterns to colour when you feel stressed (yes these do exist!)

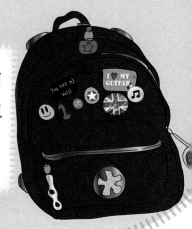

Blog Spot

'When I first heard about mindfulness and getting present, I didn't really understand it. I tried it and I am amazed as it has really helped me. I try the walking and focusing when I walk to school but the thing that helped me most was the exercise to do at the beginning of lessons I hate (page 86).'

Kaaren, 15

Flabby Brain   Toned Brain

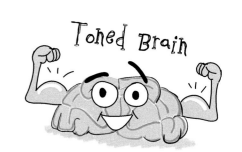

The smirch knows what humans are like...

and how easy it is to distract you or get you overthinking again. So, this is something you have to work at in order to start feeling the benefits. We are not like our pets, we can choose to use our brain three which they don't have, to notice and change our bad habits of drifting into our heads worrying, planning, thinking, daydreaming, envying and regretting.

Here are a few of my favourite ideas to tone your present moment part of the brain:

1. Think of something you do often...
like: get dressed, use the toilet, have a drink, hold a steering wheel, do up a zip or comb your hair. Use this activity as a reminder and each time you do it, notice five things you can see and hear.

2. When you are walking on your own...
decide that you will use just a couple of minutes to pay attention: What are you passing? Who do you pass? Do they look happy or sad? What pleasant things can you smell? Can you hear anything?

3. Pay attention to your breathing for five minutes...
Sit or lie down and just pay attention to the sound and feelings of your breathing. Notice where you can most feel your breathing and focus there, notice as you breathe in and out.

4. Eat the first mouthful of each meal...
as though you have never tasted it before. Look at it before it goes in your mouth and notice what happens in your mouth by just looking at it. Notice its shape and colour, smell it and really take the time to breathe in the aroma. Put it in your mouth and take a few moments before you bite into it. Feel its texture on your tongue, then bite into it noticing what you taste and what it feels like. Try this with one square of your favourite chocolate.

5. Get a book of patterns to colour...
and really focus on what you are doing—the colour, the marks the pen makes and staying within the lines.

SCIENCE FACT

You can re-wire your brain by learning present moment techniques as your brain changes depending on how it's used. People who spend a lot of time caught up in their heads feel more stressed and less mentally well than people who learn to spend more time paying attention to the present.

Blog Spot

'When I feel panicky in a car, I do some belly breaths and then choose five things I can see and hear.'

Matthew, 13

Practice Ideas

Simply notice what you are doing: eating, phone checking, self harming, crying. Ask yourself, what am I doing, why am I doing that? Is it helpful?

6. When you sit down in a lesson you hate...

or with people you feel uncomfortable with, notice what your breathing is like. Notice the environment—what you can hear, smell, see and notice—where the chair touches your body. Push your feet to the floor and notice what your feet feel, then take a deep breath and really pay attention to the teacher or someone else. What is he/she wearing? Do they look relaxed or tense? Who are they watching? Notice the way their body shape changes as they move and the different shadows they create. Watch their mouth and really listen to what they are saying.

7. Choose an activity you do every day...

like packing your bag or walking to school and write down how you did that activity in as much detail as you can—what you can see, smell, the sequence of what you do. Pretend you are going to be cross-examined on the detail. Do it every day for a week, each day notice more and more detail.

> Write in your journal as many examples as you can of when you practised being in the present moment using all your senses. Search the internet for more mindfulness and present moment ideas and videos!

Be present and mindful when you listen to others

Really concentrate on listening rather than letting your mind wander or thinking what you will say. If you can stay in the moment, it will really help your relationships and make you more attractive.

Choose one of these things as your today goal:

I will walk and deliberately notice the sensations of my body moving.

I will take a shower and notice the sensations of water on my body.

I will pay attention to sounds such as clocks ticking, birds chirping or cars passing.

I will notice the smells in the rooms I use.

You will need to practise getting present as much as you can. No one will ever be able to perfect it but this is a big smirch shrinking ability and it's worth trying for an A* in present moment studies.

Ask an adult

Choose an adult who seems to be stressed and show them how to get into the present moment using their senses. Practise the eating exercise at a family meal time and talk about how it feels to savour the first mouthful.

> 'It sounds easy to pay attention but it is easier to get hooked back into my head listening to my smirch talk about what other people are saying and thinking. It's harder than it sounds but I am going to practise as I like the idea of training my brain to be calmer.'
>
> Oscar, 15

Blog Spot

Shrinking tip 11 Grow your confidence

The smirches love people with low confidence...

as they are easier to pick on. Your smirch knows that when you are feeling anxious you will be easier to intimidate. As you grow in confidence, the smirch shrinks.

Are you a confident person? Yes or No?

Here is a short test to see how confident you are. Tick the things that you can do with confidence:

Turn on a light ☐   Walk ☐   Eat using cutlery ☐   Use a phone ☐

Get dressed ☐   Look in a mirror ☐   Shower ☐

Check out what you scored:

0-2 you lack confidence   **2-5 you are averagely confident**   **5-7 you are super confident**

You are probably thinking that this is a ridiculous test.

I expect your mind smirch is saying, 'everyone can do those things, they are easy.' But what happens if you ask a baby to do those seven things? They will fail! Is that because they lack confidence? No! It's because they have not yet learnt those skills. Ask your parents how it was when you walked and dressed yourself for the first time. They will say you fell, you struggled and you failed time and time again until finally you did it! You stood up and walked or you finally put on your school uniform without help. They will probably also tell you how pleased you were with yourself as that's the reward for learning a new skill. It makes you feel you can do it, you can trust yourself to succeed, confidence grows.

There is no such thing as a confident person!

We are all confident with the things we can do well. Perhaps you find it hard to:

Speak in class

Talk to new people

Take exams

Say no to smirchins

Apply for a job

Drive

Go to parties

Read and write

Do physical activities

However, all these things are just skills you can learn like: getting dressed, turning on a light and using a phone. The smirch wants you to do nothing but stay under your duvet in a dark room listening to its songs.

Perhaps you want to ask a teacher something about your homework or talk to a new person or join a Zumba class. The smirch thinks 'oh no, this will grow their confidence and shrink my power so I had better write some good lyrics to play.' It plugs in the smirchipod, turns up the volume and plays:

Smirch lie

'Confidence is like eye colour, you have blue eyes or you don't, nothing you can do if you have brown eyes and no confidence.'

You Will fail
Others will laugh
She will Be Better
You always mess stuff up
You are not confident enough yet

The Smirch songs make you feel afraid and if you listen to these unhelpful lyrics you will stay at home, not speak and not learn anything new. Happy smirch, less confidence for you and no feeling of pleasure at having achieved what you wanted. What a bully this smirch is.

SCIENCE FACT

Important confidence fact: Confidence is not doing things without feeling afraid, it is doing things even though you feel afraid.

Think of someone you admire for doing something well.

Is it a singer? Or your mum baking? Or maybe your friend playing sport? If you look hard, you will see they are really paying attention to the task, they are **PRESENT.**

The mistake we make when we look at others is we believe they are confident in what they are doing. But even amazing performers or brilliant athletes say that before they do their thing, they feel anxious, afraid, sick etc. It's what humans feel when they are faced with a challenge and if you don't do anything until you feel confident you won't do anything ever. The smirch **WILL** be happy.

DO Something.

Confidence comes after action, not before.

Try this.

- Choose a situation where you lack confidence.
- Accept when you try and do it, you will have feelings you don't like.
- Do it anyway, do it again, and again and again.
- Get present, really focus on the thing you are doing.
- Think about how a confident person would do that task and act like that.
- Remember, no one can see your tricky thoughts and feelings.
- Then choose another challenge.

Just think: if you had waited to walk and get dressed until you felt confident, you would still be sitting naked on your mum's lap, now there is a scary thought!

If being uncertain makes you worried...

the best way to cope is to learn to deal with the feeling of 'not knowing if it will be OK'. Don't keep asking others for reassurance, it just feeds the smirch. Learn to trust your own judgement and to experience the anxiety that comes with not asking. If you feel anxious this means you are doing the right thing to shrink your smirch!

Notice when you are asking others what they think and make a today goal like:

- Giving in homework without getting it checked.
- Ordering new food or drink at a cafe.
- Not asking the opinions of others about new clothes or what to wear.

Watch your body language, stand like you are confident, don't slouch, look at people when you are talking or listening.

Don't label yourself or let others say you are under-confident, that's smirch talk.

Write a list of the things you can do with confidence, however small.

> The smirch says **FEAR** stands for
> **F**orget **E**verything **A**nd **R**un
>
> but let **FEAR** mean
> **F**ace **E**verything **A**nd **R**ejoice

Don't listen to unhelpful smirch songs...

after you have tried something new like 'well you messed that up, they were all staring and laughing'. Just think, NBPS, I am growing and you are shrinking. In the words of a famous sports brand, 'just do it!'

Practice Ideas

Volunteer for a few hours a month. People who give their time helping others are more confident than others.

Learn something new, learn to bake a cake, play an instrument or how to say 'shrinking the smirch' in Filipino. The internet allows you to learn practically anything in your own room.

Each day set yourself a small challenge to push you outside of your comfort zone like: get a stranger to smile, say 'hello' to an older person, ask the checkout assistant if they are having a nice day, give a teacher a compliment, take a carrier bag to school, wear no make up or rubbish trainers, misuse a word when talking or cross out something rather than do the work again. Notice how pleased with yourself you feel when you do your challenge.

Chapter 6: Smirch Shrinking Habits

Have a look in Your Bag!

You now know your values and have four vital shrinking tips (see chapter 4) and good ideas for managing your tricky thoughts and feelings so you can spend more time in the present moment enjoying your life. Your smirch is beginning to lose confidence and if you are using the 'practice ideas' you may already be feeling a little better.

Habits are managed in the lizard brain and are things you do time and time again without thinking so they are easy to learn but hard to break. This brings good and bad news, bad because we all have negative habits that we wish we could stop but good because if we develop positive habits, they are also hard to break.

This chapter includes four habits: Two Ps and two Gs.
Three are good habits that if you practise will help you for the rest of your life. The fourth habit is gadget use, which is a fun thing that the smirch will try and make into a bad habit, so be careful.

Shrinking tip 12 Two 'Ps'

Planning and Problem Solving

Examples of Bad habits

Smoking, shouting at others, harming yourself, being spiteful

Examples of good habits

Saying 'please', getting dressed, washing your hands, using the toilet

Two good habits to start now and keep for life are **planning** and **problem solving.**

For your bag

Sections in your journal for planning and problem solving

Planning Sheet

Activity	Time start	Time finish	Rest/ Activity	Don't forget
Getting up/ shower	7.30	8.00	A	
Breakfast	8.00	8.30	R	
Pack bag and plan day	8.30	8.45	A	
School registration	9.00	9.15	A	
1st lesson	9.15	10.15	A	Remember science homework
break	10.15	10.30	R	
Lesson 3/4	10.30	12.30	A	
Lunch	12.30	1.30	R	Meet up with Dave
Lesson 4/5	1.30	3.30	A	
School finishes! Get bus	3.30	4.00	R	Meet Oscar
Do homework/ chores	4.00	4.45	A	
Chill and watch TV	4.45	5.30	R	
Dinner with family	5.30	6.15	A	
Help clear up	6.15	6.30	A	
Hobby time	6.30	7.00	R	
Youth group	7.00	8.00	A	Take money for snack
Brush teeth, PJs	8.15	8.30	A	
Read then sleep	8.30	9.00	R	

Planning

The smirch knows that a good way to make you stressed and to keep you out of the present is to provide a constant whirl of information to spin in your head. It plays tunes about all the things you have to do and the problems you have to solve. It knows you won't be able to concentrate with all this information cluttering up your head space and that you will soon start to forget things, feel chaotic and panic. It's like your head is a washing machine on the spin setting or a smart gadget with too many open apps. The battery gets drained.

Then your smirch plays some lyrics such as 'perhaps you are insane', 'maybe you are ill', 'you are not coping'. The smirch is happy when you feel totally paralysed and overwhelmed by the demands placed on you.

SCIENCE FACT

CONFIDENTIAL TOP SECRET CONFIDENTIAL

Most behaviours take three weeks to become a habit. It takes the same amount of time to break a habit. You need practice and determination to make or break a habit.

All You need is...

a piece of paper or a section in your journal where you can write the times and things you intend to do. On page 56, Shrinking Tip 3 you can see a good example of a detailed plan.

You may only have time to jot down a few scribbled notes on a scrap of paper or write a list on your phone but make sure every day you don't leave the house until you know what you need to prioritise.

'Fail to plan, plan to fail'

is a well-known phrase that smirches don't like as it tells of a useful lifeline. Smirches thrive on chaos and hate structure, routine and planning because they know this helps everyone. Planning each day is a good habit and will help you in so many ways. Planning will help focus your attention. It will free up your mind from all the things whirring in your head and make you less likely to forget or feel stressed.

Try this

Sit down in the morning or last thing at night and decide what you will do and when. Remind yourself of any appointments you must remember and allocate them to the time. Don't forget to mark in enough time for travelling without a rush and also note anything you need to take with you. Include a balance of rest, work and fun. Plan regular food and water as this helps you concentrate. Make sure each day that you include things that give you a sense of achievement, contact with others and that make you happy.

Planning Sheet

Activity	Time start	Time finish	Rest/ Activity	Don't forget
Getting up/ shower	7.30	8.00	A	
Breakfast	8.00	8.30	R	
Pack bag and plan day	8.30	8.45	A	
School registration	9.00	9.15	A	
1st lesson	9.15	10.15	A	
break	10.15	10.30	R	
Lesson 3/4	10.30	12.30	A	Remember science homework
Lunch	12.30	1.30	R	
Lesson 4/5	1.30	3.30	A	
School finished/ Get bus	3.30	4.00	A	Meet up with Dave
Do homework/ chores	4.00	4.45	A	Meet Oscar
Chill and watch TV	4.45	5.30	R	
Dinner with family	5.30	6.15	A	
Help clear up	6.15	6.30	A	
Hobby time	6.30	7.00	R	
Youth group	7.00	8.00	A	Take money for snack
Brush teeth, PJs	8.15	8.30	A	
Read then sleep	8.30	9.00	R	

When Your head feels fit to Burst...

the smirch feels strong and you feel like running away or going to bed. List the things that are bothering you. Include the small things and the bigger ones. Use the notes app on your phone or use pen and paper to spill out the contents of your head.

Practice Ideas

When you have finished your plan for the day, ask yourself, would this be a reasonable plan to ask a friend to follow? Don't put in so much that you will fail.

Problem solving

The smirches like you to feel overwhelmed with all your problems muddled together. They make sure they keep it all going round in your head unsolved so you feel anxious and fearful. Every day we have to make heaps of decisions and solve problems large and small to ensure all goes well, when to get up, what to eat, who to text, what to learn, how to get to college, what time to go to bed etc.

Blog Spot

'I found planning useful because I could set a goal and a plan for the next day which helped me feel more organised.'

Katy, 18

'Planning the day ahead helped me to feel in control and know what I have to do.'

Jess, 19

Blog Spot

Sometimes a problem or decision gets stuck and goes round and round taking up all your headspace. The smirches love those days. It may be a small problem or a massive decision:

I got asked to a party my parents won't like, should I go?

Which university should I go to?

How can I tell my friend she is being hurtful?

What should I do when I leave school?

What shall I wear to the cinema?

Should I look for a Saturday job?

How can I end a relationship?

What do I eat for lunch?

Shall I use all my money to buy that expensive bag?

Blog Spot

'I tried this problem solving way to decide whether or not to carry on doing German, I had been thinking and thinking for ages and it was really messing with me head. Writing all the pros and cons helped a lot and I could show my parents and German teacher to prove I had thought it out.'

Lee, 16

Whatever the issue the same five problem solving steps can be used. If you practise, it will become a habit and you will be able to use it quickly in your head. This will really help you in life.

Here is how to solve a problem in 5 easy steps

1 Problem statement

Write the problem in clear words so anyone could understand what you mean.

2 Problem details

Ask yourself the following questions: Who is involved in this problem? What makes this a problem?

3 Possible solutions

Think of as many solutions as possible even if they aren't sensible!

4 Pros and cons of each solution

Look at each possible solution and think about what the positives and negatives would be of using that solution. Ask others what they think too.

5 Pick the best solution or solutions

Does it fit with your values? Ask yourself how you will feel after you have acted upon your decision. An example is shown below.

Problem Statement

I want to go to a party but my parents don't want me to as there will be free alcohol, no adults and it's in a rough area.

Solutions:
1. Stay home, feel like a loser.
2. Go to the party and upset my parents.
3. Go to the party and lie to my parents.
4. Talk to parents calmly about their worries.
5. Go somewhere else.
6. Stay in and invite other friends for film.
7. Compromise, go for two hours then ask parents to collect me.
8. Run away.
9. Go but tell everyone I am on medication so I can't drink.
10. Go and get plastered.
11. Scream at my parents for being so unreasonable.

Solution 1: Stay home: pros and cons

Cons

- Feel like a loser.
- Feel left out.
- Smirch tells me I will be rejected.
- Regret not going.
- Party host will be mean to me.

Pros

- Parents happy.
- No temptations.
- Save money on present.
- I can remind myself thoughts and feelings can be managed.
- Save energy as shattered.
- Could do something else nice.

Do this for each solution.

Chosen solution: talked to two friends who also were not really allowed to go, stayed in, watched a film and ate pizza, was a really nice evening actually.

Review in your journal if the decision was right. If not, what would you have done differently? Think through some problems and decisions you have struggled with and use the problem solving steps to help you make the right choice.

Shrinking tip 13 Two 'Gs'

Gadgets and Gratitude

This shrinking tip is about noticing a bad habit but also learning another good habit. The smirch wants you to keep wanting more and more and more, more things, more friends, more likes. The smirch knows social media is a great tool to make you unsatisfied and ungrateful and that's how smirches want you to be: always craving everything you haven't got and wanting to do everything you can't.

Smirches love gadgets and screens even more than young people as they know smart gadgets can be useful mind enemies, just like them. I am sure you know about the dangers of cyber bullying, false identities and online fraud but smirches know the biggest problem with social media is it feeds anxiety, and keeps young people in reptile mode: restless and hissing.

For your bag

1. A SMART goal for managing social media.

2. A gratitude section for your journal.

3. Smiley stickers to stick everywhere to remind you to smile and be grateful.

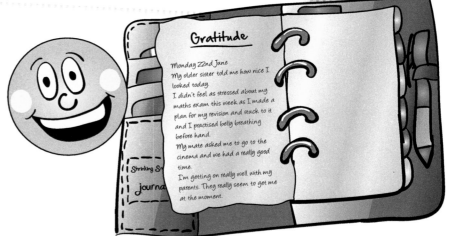

Gratitude

Monday 22nd June
My older sister told me how nice I looked today.
I didn't feel as stressed about my maths exam this week as I made a plan for my revision and stuck to it and I practised belly breathing before hand.
My mate asked me to go to the cinema and we had a really good time.
I'm getting on really well with my parents. They really seem to get me at the moment.

Here are a few things smirches love to watch:

The disappointment in the morning when the number of likes or retweets on posts is not enough.

People missing their life while taking photos or checking everyone else's life.

People not enjoying food after posting a picture of the delicious looking dish on Instagram.

People not enjoying the last episode of their favourite programme to make sure they are the first to comment about the results.

Everyone rushing off to take selfies in the toilet so others realise the fun they are having.

Young people turning down activities with real people to stay in a virtual world.

All these things are great ideas for new smirch songs

'You are not good enough.'

'Everyone else has more fun than you.'

'You are left out, boring and dull.'

'You never have fun.'

G is for Gadgets

Smart gadgets, gaming and social media can be great fun and give many benefits that older people didn't enjoy when they were young. Without leaving your bedroom you can chat with people in many different places, play games and get instant information.

BUT what the smirches are loving is that people are addicted to the screens and are spending more time trying to **LOOK** happy and fun than they are actually **BEING** happy and having fun.

Are You an addict?

(Try this experiment to find out.)

Hide all your gadgets for a day: phone/laptop/ tablet/gaming equipment. Then answer truthfully, did you:

- Think about your gadgets more than five times in the day?

- Feel anxious, fearful, upset or insecure?

- Think about what you were missing, worry about what was going on?

- Feel restless?

- Feel bored?

- Feel angry?

- Have any strong urges to give in and retrieve gadgets?

- Experience a massive sense of relief when the gadgets come back out?

If you answered yes to two or more of these questions, you are probably addicted to gadgets and/or social media and your smirch just **LOVES** it.

Addictions are...

habits that take up all your thoughts and make you behave in a way that damages your physical or mental health. Something has become a bad habit or even an addiction if you feel anxious, irritable and paranoid when you can't do it. The smirch knows that it can just grab a deck chair and chill if people are addicted to gaming and social media as addiction is as good a mind enemy as a smirch.

The smirches love screens as they know excessive gadget use:

- Stops useful activity like studying or real life talking.
- Makes you afraid and unable to relax when you are on your own.
- Causes both physical and mental health problems.
- Keeps your brain in reptile mode: anxious and restless as you constantly check them.

FOR THOUGHT

Researchers at Chicago University concluded that social media addiction can be stronger than addiction to cigarettes and alcohol following an experiment in which they recorded the cravings of several hundred people for several weeks. Media cravings ranked ahead of cravings for cigarettes and alcohol.

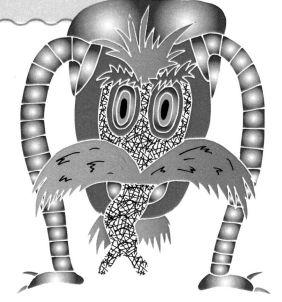

Smirch lie

'Everyone is having more fun than you.'

SCIENCE FACT

Many people check their phones up to 150 times a day. There is now even a name for excessive phone use: 'infomania'. Are you an infomaniac?!

Instead of getting into Battles with teachers and parents about social media and screens, **STOP and NOTICE!** Ask yourself five questions and write the honest answers in your journal.

1. Does checking or posting on social media make me feel better?

2. If yes, for how long?

3. Does it shrink or grow my smirch?

4. How do I feel when I have spent a long time gaming or staring at screens?

5. Am I missing out on anything due to my constant need to be near a screen?

Addiction to screens

Think about the answers and decide if you need to make a SMART or 'today' goal about your gaming and social media habits. Tell someone else your goal.

Smirch lie

'If you don't check your phone, you will miss something important.'

Blog Spot

'I hadn't realised how constantly checking my phone made me feel. I noticed I couldn't relax without my phone near me. I tried three hours each day without my phone for a week and it was horrible and I didn't think I would cope, but on the third day I actually enjoyed doing other things. By the last day I was looking forward to a phone break - weird I know.'

Lillian, 16

Try these things and note the results in your journal

- Agree a week of no screens at meal times, see what happens

- Choose several times a day when you will switch off your screens for a set time, even 10 to 15 minutes can help you achieve more and feel less stressed

- Ask an adult to have a gadget fast. Yes, they are often as bad

- Have a good long social media session, check and post as you usually do. Now stop and have a good objective look at your mind and body. Go into curious scientist mode and notice whether you are relaxed or tense, feeling content and grateful or not good enough. Ask yourself if the social media session has taken you closer to who you want to be. Write in your journal any observations

- Designate 'no-device zones' like the dining room or car; even the Obamas leave their phones in a basket outside the kitchen

- Download an app to count how many times you check your phone each day

'I don't have any social media accounts. It makes life less stressful.'

Blog Spot

Katy, 18

'I have stopped taking so many photos as I realised I was missing the present moment and sort-of living in a second-hand life!'

Blog Spot

Max, 18

'I noticed some people's posts made me feel rubbish and insecure. I de-friended those people. I also decided I wouldn't check my phone after 9pm as it gets in my head and I can't sleep.'

Blog Spot

Kylie, 15

FOOD FOR THOUGHT

In America and Europe the smartest doctors and scientists are recommending you don't spend more than two hours a day gaming. They have found using it more can make you more likely to have a heart attack when you are older.

G is for Gratitude

Gratitude is a good habit which is the perfect antidote to the feelings of dissatisfaction that are fed by social media.

When children are very small, one of the things parents ask them many times is: 'what do you say?' They are waiting for a 'thank you'.

The smirches hate good manners and love to be rude and ignorant. They try and make young people feel like that too. They play tunes like:

'Everyone else has one.'   'All my friends are allowed.'   'It's not fair.'   'Why can't I have one of those?'   'Gimme more stuff!'

These lyrics make young people feel like their life is rubbish and it will only get better if they get more stuff and are allowed to do more things.

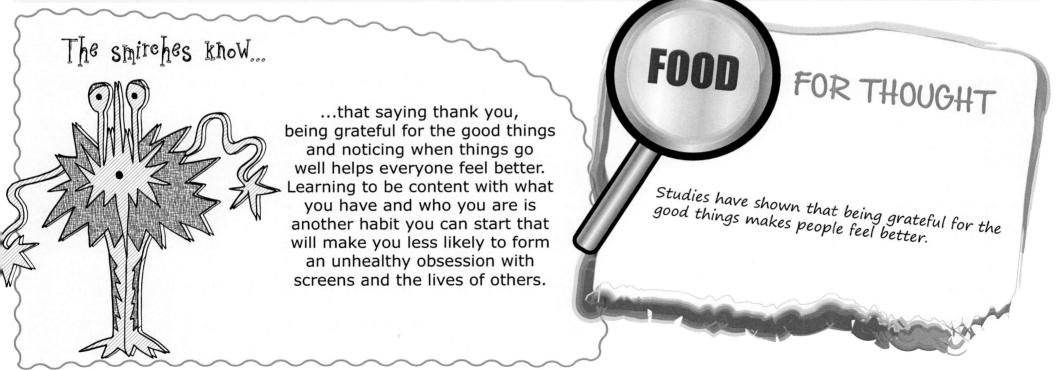

The smirches know...

...that saying thank you, being grateful for the good things and noticing when things go well helps everyone feel better. Learning to be content with what you have and who you are is another habit you can start that will make you less likely to form an unhealthy obsession with screens and the lives of others.

FOOD FOR THOUGHT

Studies have shown that being grateful for the good things makes people feel better.

The problem is that human brains are flawed and what they do very easily is:

- Point out all the bad stuff.
- Notice the things that go wrong.
- Remember the nasty things that are said.
- Think about the worst.
- Notice what they haven't got.

So we remember...

the teacher who was mean and the friend who said something unkind, but we forget the 'laugh we had at lunchtime' or the fact it was sunny. The research shows that if you try harder to look for the good stuff, the brain gets better at noticing when things go well, which over time makes you feel better.

Someone once said happiness is like your favourite perfume. It still smells as good as when you first smelt it but you have got used to it so it doesn't grab your conscious attention, you don't notice.

FOOD FOR THOUGHT

You can't be happy if you are giving out anger or hatred to others.

The smirch wants you...

to be thinking and wishing for all the things you don't have but not to notice the good things you do have. Check back to the first shrinking tip. What are the important things and who would be the important people if you had only a week to live? These are the things and people you need to notice and be grateful for.

Practice Ideas

Each evening write down down five things that went well today or that you are grateful for. It could be big things like a lovely gift, a success or really small things like a nice thing someone said or finding 10p. Use your journal. Do it for five days and see what happens.

SCIENCE FACT

TOP SECRET
CONFIDENTIAL

Smile at a smirch! If you behave as if you are happy, sit up straight and smile for 15 to 30 seconds, the brain thinks you are happy and you feel happier. Put up stickers of smiley faces at home and at work to remind you to smile.

Blog Spot

'I think I will try and notice positive things more. It helped change my perspective sometimes - I could see that the afternoon may not have been as bad as it felt.'

Ed, 17

Ask an adult

what they are grateful for today and if anything good came out of any difficult experiences they have had.

Challenge them to do 100 days of happy photos.

Practice Ideas

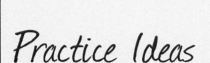

For a 100 days take a photo of something that made you happy. At the end look at the happy photos and explain them to a friend or family member. You could make a scrapbook of all your happy days.

Blog Spot

'I thought that the gratitude task was good, but five things was a lot of things that went well in one day. I was able to write down things most days, but still not five good things, only about three. It got easier to do over the week. These are some of my good things: I understood maths one day, someone said they like my eyeliner, I had a good lunch, I got paid at work and my biology test went well. I will continue this activity because when I read back over it, it makes me feel happy and shows a good balance.'

Johanna, 16

Strange But True

This might seem strange but research tells us that people can even find good things when life is hard or something terrible has happened in your life or family. Smirches know that bad feelings, being ill and even grief can strangely be quite good for people's minds and relationships.

When bad stuff is happening, the questions the smirches most dread you asking are:

'Could this bring anything positive?'

'How might this experience help me get closer to the person I want to be?'

'What practical skills might I learn or improve?'

Of course if you start thinking about these questions the smirch will not be happy and it will find some negative lyrics to play: 'Don't be so stupid!' 'How can this be good?' 'This can only get worse.' 'Why me?' 'Nothing good will ever happen to me.'

If you read what you have written in your journal after a few months you might find that it is easier to stay close to your values when you are having a tough time as we know that difficult experiences often allow people to show their inner strength and it becomes easier to see what is really important.

Practice Ideas

Think of someone you are glad of in your life. Write a short letter or thank you card for them.

Blog Spot

'My mum got cancer and I was so frightened but it made me realise my family are way more important than my friends and I need to treat them better. It reminded me of a bible verse that says this: suffering produces perseverance, character and hope.'

Kaaren, 15

Blog Spot

'My friend fell over and broke her leg. I was devastated as I had to go to the prom on my own but I was kind to her and realised I could control my feelings of wanting to be angry with her as I wanted to be a good friend.'

Sarah, 16

Blog Spot

'I assumed that it would be pretty easy to find 5 positive points in one day as it seems like nothing. I managed to do it everyday this week but I actually found it quite difficult. I found it a little easier with each day. I will definitely try to continue doing it every evening because it really helped me have a more positive outlook, which I know I often struggle with, and it helped to take my mind off any low points during the day and instead pick out the good parts which made me feel a lot happier and optimistic overall.

Here are some positive things that happened in my week: my parents taking me out to dinner, a friend complimenting my skirt, a positive driving lesson, playing a good netball match in the sun, and a friend offering me help with a business essay.'

Katie, 17

Chapter 7: Body Stuff

In this section we are looking at a number of physical health issues:

- **What you put in your mouth**
- **How much you move**
- **How much you chill**

Your journal will be key to defeating your smirch in these areas.

Each issue is different but some key principles apply to all. **You can remember these principles as the 3 As**

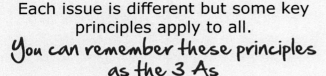

3 Act

Choose a SMART or 'today' goal to help you do less of the unhelpful things and more of the things that keep your mind and body healthy.

2 Analyse

Use the journal to work out how each health issue links to your good and bad days and the size of your smirch. Look for patterns, eg *'When I get the balance right between rest and work, my smirch is smaller.' 'When I eat well, I feel brighter.' 'When I drink too much, I am more likely to self harm.'*

1 Assess

This is where you keep detailed notes about what is happening. Put space in your journal to record food, mood, water, alcohol, substances, exercise and rest etc.

Shrinking tip 14 Exhaust your smirch

Smirches are very lazy

They like to irritate young people with little effort. They know that humans are easy targets when they are alone, doing nothing and caught up in their heads. Smirches find sweat very unpleasant and so if you are active they will stay away. They also like to laze about and not move, so if you are moving you already have more power than the smirch.

A pedometer or a step counting app like 'pacer

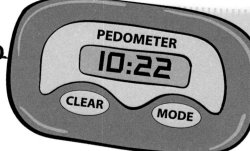

PEDOMETER

10:22

CLEAR   MODE

FOOD FOR THOUGHT

Exercising causes the body to produce endorphins, chemicals that can help a person to feel more peaceful and happy.

Twenty minutes of exercise three times a week (even walking) is better for mild depression than medication.

Experts recommend that teenagers get 60 minutes of exercise every day.

Smirches know that physical activity has lots of amazing side effects.
Exercise improves lots of body functions but also helps thinking and memory, so exercise could even improve your grades! No wonder smirches hate people exercising. They will try all their top songs to try and keep you still. *'You are too fat/anxious/cool to exercise'*, *'you will feel terrible'*, *'it will make your tiredness worse'*, *'people will stare at you'*.

Beware! They will fight this battle hard as they know that even a little more moving can make you feel so much better in your body and mind.

If you notice and get present as you move...

this will be even more beneficial to your mind and body, and so moving more will then have a double shrinking value.

Remember the 3 As principles

Assess

How much are you moving?
Keep a record of how much activity you do in a day. Maybe a pedometer will help to count your steps or just note activity in your journal.

Analyse

How does activity affect your life?
Perhaps you are not moving enough or overdoing it some days and staying in bed on others.

Act

Set a SMART or 'today' goal about exercise.
For example: 'I am going to stop using exercise to suppress bad feelings.'
'I am going to walk to college on Mondays and Fridays.'

Practice Ideas

- Choose the right type of exercise, consider your exercise personality. For example, if you like to exercise alone, sports like cycling or walking may be for you but if it helps to be with others you might want to join a team, go to an exercise class or go swimming or ice skating with friends.
- Get a friend or an unfit parent to commit to a regular fun activity that requires moving.

When exercise grows the smirch!

As with gadgets, it's possible to overdo exercise. The body needs enough calories to function properly. This is especially true for teenagers who are still growing. Exercising too much to lose weight isn't healthy and can be a sign of an eating disorder. If you ever get the feeling that your exercise is in charge of you rather than the other way around, make sure you tell an adult you trust.

Shrinking tip 15
Notice what goes into the hole under your nose

For your bag

A food and mood section in your journal

The smirch loves alcohol, drugs and junk food!

These things change the way your brain works, making you care less about what you say and do and increasing bad feelings.

If you have feelings of anxiety, anger or unhappiness, the smirch knows unhealthy habits make these feelings seem much worse, which is why most smirches play these songs:

It will help you cope.   Go on have a drink.

It makes you feel better,   Smoke some weed.

Binge on junk food.   It makes you more sociable.

FAT!

Smirches know...

that these things only numb bad feelings for a short time and that the feelings of anxiety and depression will be even worse when the effects wear off. Smirches don't really care whether people are fat, thin or in-between, but they do care a lot about mood. They know that a few days or weeks of consistent high sugar eating or high caffeine drinks will inevitably lead to bad feelings—another of their favourite things.

The smirch wants you...

on auto-pilot—not noticing your own smirch—as it knows you will then be more likely to do things that will ruin relationships and keep you unhealthy. So you first need to flex your noticing muscle by using the three As.

So Back to the 3 As

Assess

Start to record in your journal what and when you consume anything, eg type of food, high energy drinks, alcohol, drugs, and how this changes what you think, feel and do. Try and be honest with your journal even if some of the things you are doing make you feel ashamed or upset.

Analyse

Become more aware of the patterns. Do you eat more junk food at certain times of the day or the month? Do you use food to blot out bad feelings? Do you eat too little or too infrequently? How does what you consume impact your feelings, sleep, thinking and mood that day and the day after?

Act

When you have noticed what you are doing and why, it will be easy to know what to do:

- You might need to set a 'today' goal so you become healthier. For example: *'I will drink two more glasses of water during my day'*, *'I will have one less bar of chocolate a week'*, *'I will not drink more than two cans of alcohol'* or *'when I am anxious I will try and do something else to manage my feelings before I have food.'*

- You might want to use the problem solving template to decide how to sort out the problem of drinking or eating too much (page 95).

- You might want to practise some more present moment ideas so you don't eat and drink in lizard brain auto-pilot mode (page 84-85).

- You might want to look at the section on managing tricky thoughts and feelings if that's what you are trying to get rid of (page 79-82).

- You might need to talk to an adult and get some help if you think you might have an addiction or an eating disorder (page 126-127).

Practice Ideas

Make small changes, one at a time so you can see what is working and keep it up. Smirches know it is small changes that work, small changes that can last for a lifetime, not just days.

SCIENCE FACT

CONFIDENTIAL · TOP SECRET

The most vital substance for a healthy mind and body is water. The recommended six to eight glasses per day can quickly improve how your mind and body feels.

'I realise I drink when I am sad but the next day I feel even more sad.'

Dan, 16

Blog Spot

Eat like a Great Grandma!

Eat how your great grandparents would have eaten before junk food was invented. Aim for a healthy meal at least five days a week.

'Breakfast is the most important meal of the day.'

'Keep the treats small and not every day.'

'Eat more fruit and vegetables.'

'Avoid ready meals and high sugar foods.'

'Eat many different types of food.'

'Don't go on quick-fix diets.'

Blog Spot

'At certain times in the month I just want to eat junk food, I hide it and eat and eat and make myself feel ill. It makes me feel disgusting.'

Kaaren, 15

Practice Ideas

Too much caffeine can cause symptoms of anxiety and make it hard to sleep. Caffeine is in coffee, high energy drinks and even chocolate. If you want to try and consume less caffeine, cut down gradually or you might get withdrawal symptoms like headaches and cravings.

Blog Spot

'After I smoke weed I get very moody and shout at my family. That's not who I want to be. I probably need help.'

Mark, 18

Smirch lie

'Drugs, alcohol and food make you feel better when you feel anxious.'

Did You Know?

Food changes our mood and drink changes what we think.

Shrinking tip 16 Chillax

Shhh! gadgets resting

A personal rest plan
A box for gadgets to sleep in

George Nachman describes his perceptions of a seven day week in the Chicago Tribune.

THE CHICAGO TRIBUNE

No 301/076   THE WORLD'S MOST READ NEWSPAPER

'I looked out of the window and discovered Sunday had disappeared. Nobody had swiped it exactly, [I guess he didn't know about the smirches] but something had gone. I realised that Sunday had turned into Tuesday. Out on the street, people were no longer strolling about. They had direction, a mid-week glint in their eyes that meant business. They were walking briskly in and out of shops instead of browsing quietly past the windows. The scene was as busy as your average workday. Now all seven days are workdays!'

This newspaper article was written a few years ago now but this journalist had realised an important thing: we have lost the one day a week when everyone used to stop working and rest. When your great grandparents were growing up everything closed on Sundays and so the only option was for everyone to have a day of rest and relaxation. So when your great grandparents were eating well, they were also resting well. Of course there were no computers and not much television either.

Maybe you are thinking their lives must have been very dull

But the smirches know that our minds and bodies have not been created to live like we do. Now everyone is made to feel they should be working 24/7 to get good grades and to be constantly in contact with peers through social media so there is no rest from work or people. The smirches know people need to spend time having fun and that they need to have at least one day of rest a week.

111

We have lost an agreed weekly day of rest...

and many people don't even get an hour of rest. Smirches have a well-devised set of tunes to make resting unlikely:

'Rest is for the weak.'

'You will fail your exams.'

'You will miss an important email.'

'If you just chill, whatever can you put on Facebook?'

Physical muscles need rest days to recover and get even stronger. Our minds also need rest. More work is NOT better work.

Many smirches aim to ruin your sleep.

They know this makes your mind and body cope less well with life. Everyone needs different amounts of sleep to cope, so experiment with bed and wake-up times. When you have worked out from your journal what works best, try as hard as possible to go to bed and get up at the same time. Your body likes this, the smirch will not. Smirches often play their tunes the loudest at night. Write down any issues that are on your mind before you go to bed, notice what tunes are playing, do some belly breaths and use your present moment techniques.

> *'I looked in my journal and realised I hardly ever just do nothing. I thought I did but they are the times I keep checking my phone. I also stay up really late and that makes me feel stressy and moody.'*
>
> **Kaaren, 15**

Blog Spot

1 Assess

Look at your journal and see when you are actually taking proper rest.

2 Analyse

Look for patterns as to how over-working or doing too many activities changes how you think, feel and behave.

3 Act

Aim to have more rest. If you live within a family, plan together. Choose creative activities that are refreshing and encourage relationships. Decide that at certain times of the day all gadgets will also be put to rest and out of reach of hand or mind.

Shhh! gadgets resting

Practice Ideas

Aim to have at least one half day of rest a week. If you live within a family, see if you can convince them to do the same. Put your gadgets away, watch a film or play cards or a board game. Choose creative activities that are fun and encourage real life relationships.

'I told my dad he never rests and we decided to do a four week challenge. Every Saturday afternoon we left phones and laptops at home and took turns to choose something fun to do. We have been paint balling, cycling and to the cinema. We are going to keep it going as it's been so fun.'

Ben, 17

Blog Spot

Chapter 8:
The Final Touches

Look where we have got to. You have a massive bag of smirch shrinking ideas and your smirch is feeling pretty weak. This section gives you three final ideas you will need to keep your smirch as small as it can be for the rest of your life. We are going to finish with:

- Shrink the 'smirchINs'

- Kill your smirch with kindness

- Snitch on your smirch

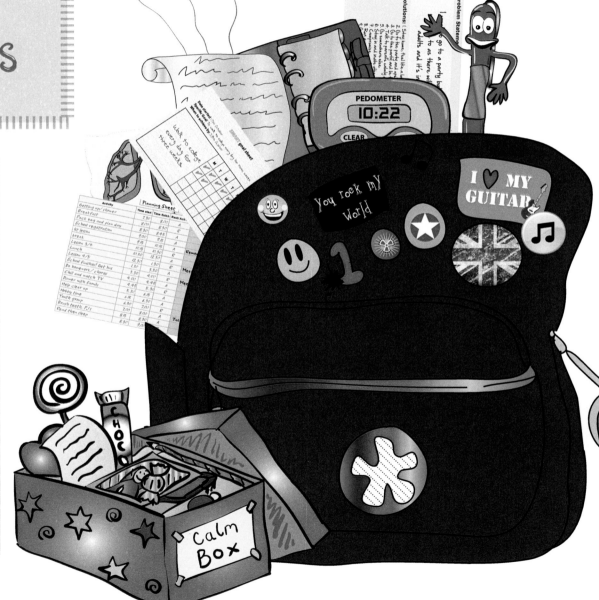

Shrinking tip 17
Shrink the 'smirchiINs': Resisting peer pressure

For your bag
A mirror to use to practise saying 'No' like you mean it.

If an object is empty, flimsy or shallow, it will be easy to break with just a little pressure applied in the right place. A thin piece of glass will shatter more easily than a solid block of wood. People are much the same. Those who are clear about their values and have practised increasing their confidence and learning some smirch shrinking techniques will be stronger. Hopefully at this point in the workbook that includes **YOU.**

Stronger people are less likely to break or be pushed when others apply pressure to behave in a way that makes them feel uncomfortable or out of line with their values.

You should have a better idea of how to make decisions on your own from Shrinking Tip 12 (page 92). When other people get involved and try to pressure you one way or another it can be harder. People who are your age are called peers. When they try to get you to do something, it's called **peer pressure.** It's something everyone has to deal with — even adults.

Ask an adult

When did you last feel pressured by others? What did you think, feel and do?

Blog Spot

'I have to look perfect all the time, make up, bag, shoes, hair. I decided to take a bag to school that I knew wasn't cool. Two of my friends said it was weird but I don't actually think anyone else noticed. That surprised me. I am doing small things like that lots of days now. It has become a bit of a game in my head and I do think my smirch has got smaller as I don't care so much about it all.'

Dionne, 15

Peer pressure can be good

You might feel pressured by a hard working friend into studying instead of gaming, you might feel pushed to return something you have stolen by your girlfriend who doesn't approve. You might exercise more because a friend you admire is good at sport. Maybe you got others excited about a great book, and now everyone's reading it.

BUT peer pressure can make you feel pushed into doing something you don't want to do...

or make you anxious you will be rejected if you don't look a certain way or wear certain clothes. Peer pressure can result in:

Buying the same clothes, shoes or jewellery as others even if you don't like them.

Wearing make up.

Listening to the same music or watching the same TV shows as others.

Changing the way you talk, or the words you use.

Taking risks or breaking rules.

Working harder at school, or not working as hard.

Taking part in sexual activities or pairing up even when you don't want to.

Smoking, drinking alcohol or using drugs.

Going to places where you feel uncomfortable.

Smirches want you to do things...

that will make you unhealthy and take you away from your values. The smirches just love it when they find humans who will help them bully people and make them feel pressured. At any age there are always some people who seem more popular and everyone else feels pressured to be like them and do what they do. They are the **SMIRCHIN** crowd. Humans who help the smirches by making others feel anxious, rejected and pressured. Only smirches know that often **SMIRCHINS** are the most anxious and insecure about being rejected and no longer being in the popular group.

'I used to look at myself every day and cry, telling my mum I was ugly as no boy asked me out. Now I realise there is so much more to me than what I look like: kindness, humour and honesty. When you realise that, people will respect you no matter what you do.'

Livvy, 19

Blog Spot

Are YOU sometimes a SmirchIN?

Do you sometimes pressure others or behave in an unkind way to make others feel rejected? There are always reasons for why people are smirchins. Perhaps you feel insecure and rubbish inside? Maybe you are being bullied or your family don't make you happy? Maybe you want to look clever or maybe you are jealous of the person you are targeting?

Go right back to 'Shrinking Tip 1' – decide who you want to be. When someone is talking truthfully about you, do you want to be known as a nasty bully, who is insecure, unkind and dishonest? Are these your values? Start to understand what your smirch is doing to make you feel like this, what voices are you hearing and what can you do to become more like the person you would like to be?

Talk to someone you trust, a teacher, a parent or a youth leader, and tell them you realise your smirch has made you feel pressured to do and say things that are not acceptable. Noticing this is very brave and will be a big step forward to becoming the adult you would prefer to be.

In order to get you to feel pressured the smirch will play you some good lyrics like:

'everyone is doing it', *'no one will find out'*, *'forget your stupid values'* or *'if you don't do it you will look like a loser'*. These songs will make you feel anxious. Peer pressure thrives on making you feel bad about yourself and makes you believe that you have to give in to feel better.

Use your journal and exercise your noticing muscles to find the answers to these questions:

Who tries to pressure me into things I don't want to do?

When do I usually get pressured?

Where am I when this happens?

Why am I giving in?

Why is the approval of this group important to me?

What will I lose if I don't gain the approval of this person?

Eleanor Roosevelt once said:

"No one can make you feel inferior without your consent"

Nine tips to shrink the peer power of the 'smirchins'

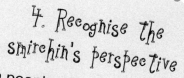

1. Be sure of your values

Check back to the first smirch shrinking tip and remind yourself of who you want to be and the people who are really important. When you feel pressured into doing something, ask yourself how you will feel after you have given in. Take a moment to think about the consequences of your actions. Think what you will feel like tomorrow or if someone you love and respect could see you. Choose friends with similar values who will support you when you don't want to do something.

4. Recognise the smirchin's perspective

Often people who pressurise others are insecure in their own views or feeling unhappy about life. Secure and happy people don't need to push others around or put them down.

3. Just say NO, NO, NO!

You always have the right to say no. No one should ever make you feel bad for not wanting to do something like have sex or take drugs or for smaller things to do with what you wear or the music you listen to. Practise saying NO like you are confident in your opinion. Make eye contact, then say 'No thanks' like you mean it and won't be persuaded. (They don't know how you feel inside!) The more certain you are in your refusal, the less people will pressure you. Practise in the mirror and with people like your family who don't make you feel insecure. When you say NO, try following it with a reason or using humour to distract. Eg if you're turning down an offer to smoke, say something like, 'I like my lungs and my gran died of lung cancer' or 'it makes my asthma worse'.

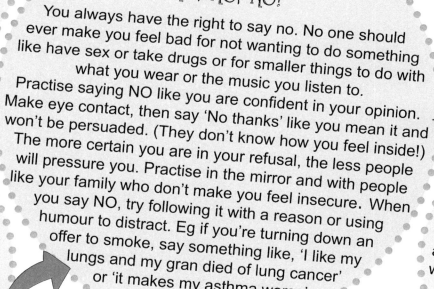

5. Use your journal

Notice the situations that make you feel most pressured and think about avoiding them. Start to notice when others are trying to force their opinion or values onto you. They may say things like 'You will LOVE this....' Or 'You need to be doing this...'

2. Grow your confidence

Use the practice ideas in Shrinking Tip 11 (page 87) to grow your confidence. The more confidence you have in yourself, the easier it will be to stand up to people trying to pressure you.

Nine tips to shrink the peer power of the smirchins

6. Look for positive role models

Notice that the successful teens at your school are the ones who weren't afraid to say what they think and feel and to follow their values. Talk to successful adults you know about how they resisted peer pressure.

7. Are they really friends?

If your peers are always pushing you into things that make you feel uncomfortable or that you will regret, perhaps these people are not friends but smirchins. Your smirch loves you being around people who make you feel bad as they don't have to work so hard. Real friends will like and respect you for who you are, not who they want you to be. Maybe it's time to search out new friends who share your values and interests.

8. It's Back to planning!

If you are going to a party or a place you know you might feel pressured by smirchins, plan in your head before you go so you won't do anything you will regret. Think of the situations that might make you feel under pressure. Imagine all the details; what people would do and say, where you are. Practise your response. Have a plan for what you would do in a situation if you start to feel uncomfortable. Choose an adult you trust and work out a code. If you text them that code word, they have to call you and say something has happened which means you need to come home. Or agree if you ever call and ask how your grandma is feeling, that means you would like help to escape a situation.

9. Get more groups

Your smirch wants you to just have one group of friends so you will do everything you can not to fall out with them even if it means doing things you don't like. Join as many groups as you can, in school and out of school. If you have lots of friends with different interests and in different places it will feel easier to resist pressure in one group. Young people who do lots of different things feel more confident in themselves and their ability to cope in challenging situations. Perhaps ask an adult to help you find what activities you might enjoy in your local area.

Smirch lie

Everyone else is doing it.

Practice Ideas

Be the person who helps when a friend is in a situation they might find difficult. This will improve your confidence as well.

Shrinking tip 18
Kill your smirch with kindness: Being kind to self

The following phrases are all found on posters displayed around schools:

Respect others

Love your neighbour as yourself

Be kind

Open doors for others

Don't be a bully, be a buddy

Most young people realise...

that living, learning and working together means having to treat others with respect or it will be more like a zoo or Smirchington High! In shrinking tip 1, lots of young people said that values like **kindness, respect** and **consideration** are important to them. When people talk about these things they are mostly thinking about how to treat others. The smirch hates it when people are kind and helpful to each other.

For your bag

A 'be kind' stone

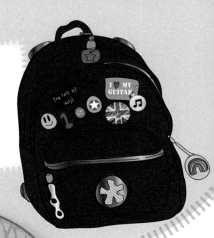

Be Kind!

SCIENCE FACT

CONFIDENTIAL TOP SECRET

Helpfulness and kindness not only help the receiver but also help the person who is being helpful and kind to feel better and that their life is worthwhile.

Blog Spot

'Sometimes a warm bath helps when I feel awful. I am trying to do this first.'

Danielle, 16

Think aBout the last time someone You love was having a hard time:

- Were they ill?
- Were they upset?
- Did they feel left out or worried?
- Or maybe they had done something they regretted?

Think back to what you said or did. Tick which statements are true:

You laughed at their misery. ◯

You gave them a carrier bag of junk food and said, 'eat that until you feel ill'. ◯

You bashed them round the head and said, 'you are such an idiot!' ◯

You gave them a blade and insisted they cut themselves. ◯

You gave them a bottle of vodka and made them drink it all. ◯

You gave them some homework and said, 'work more you useless person!' ◯

You said, 'shut up talking about this, you are so boring and stupid!' ◯

Find out Your friend score: (Tick the statement which is true)

◯ **5 - 7 You are a rubbish friend**

◯ **3- 5 You are not a great friend**

◯ **1 - 2 You could do better**

◯ **0 You are a great friend, I wish I knew you!**

SCIENCE FACT
CONFIDENTIAL TOP SECRET

Research has shown a link between the "feel-good" brain chemical dopamine and kindness. Acting with kindness increases the flow of dopamine within the do-gooder's brain, making them feel happy!

On page 47 some young people said they would want a good friend to be:

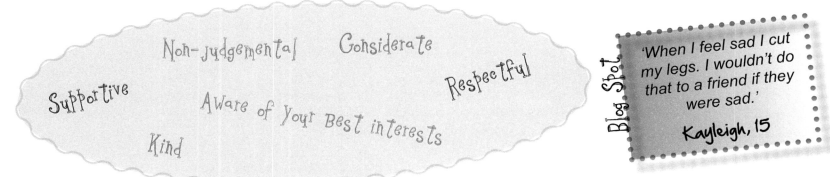

Non-judgemental   Considerate
Supportive   Aware of your best interests   Respectful
Kind

'When I feel sad I cut my legs. I wouldn't do that to a friend if they were sad.'

Kayleigh, 15

'I get really angry a lot and I am getting better at seeing it come and if I go for a run it is better than shouting at people and then beating myself up because I regret that.'

Lee, 17

Most young people try hard to be a good friend to others.

So when someone is upset, ill or hurt you might:

Give them a hug	Say kind things	Tell them it doesn't matter	Reassure them	Remind them we all make mistakes	Do something nice	Give them a present

These things will make them feel better, less lonely and more able to cope.

An odd question? How do you treat yourself?

The smirch is a bully and is great at encouraging you to listen to its unkind and spiteful songs. So when you are hurting, upset or have failed, do you hear a voice in your head that says *'I can't believe you said that, what an idiot, you have done it again, you are such a failure, you will never learn, loser, everyone is laughing and staring at you'*?

Can you see the difference? When your friend is hurting or has made a mistake you are kind and they feel better **BUT** maybe when you are in the same situation, hurting, lonely or upset, you turn up the smirch songs.

How Would Your friend feel...

if you made them listen to spiteful smirch lyrics on a bad day? The smirch loves it when you are unkind to yourself as it knows it will feed its favourite loop: think bad things, feel bad things, do bad things. So you say to yourself: You are a loser, fat, ugly, everyone hates you and is laughing. This will make you feel horrible, sad, lonely and upset and then you will most likely do something that takes you away from your values. Maybe you will stay alone, hide your feelings, drink too much, hurt yourself or shout at people you like.

Go back to the friendship questionnaire on page 121 and score how you treat yourself when you are hurting. Could you do better as a self friend? Can you can learn to be a good friend to yourself? Well that **IS** a weird idea! BUT there is good evidence that you can stop being a self bully and learn to be nicer to yourself. This will help you and make it more likely that you can stick with your values too.

Very Young children...

are unkind most of the time to others: they are spiteful, they hit and take. If you no longer do this to your friends, then you have learnt to be a good friend. In the same way you have to learn to be a good friend to **yourself**. It takes practice as most young people are self bullies but you just have to do **FOUR** things:

1. Notice when you feel upset, sad or angry	**2. Think about what you are saying to yourself**	**3. Take some belly breaths**	**4. When you feel bad, think of something that you find comforting or helpful and get it for yourself. Eg**
Take some deep breaths and see if you can say something nice to yourself like 'poor you, you are feeling rubbish'. Sometimes you might know why but often bad feelings can come from nowhere, it's just a bad day.	Ask yourself the BF question. Would I treat my best friend like this when he/she was feeling bad? Try and think what you would say to your friend and say that to yourself. If you notice you are saying nasty things to yourself say, 'that's not a very nice thing to say' as if you were saying it to a young child who was being a bully.	Practise one of the basic present moment techniques on page 85. REMEMBER: we are all flawed humans and all young people feel bad and mess up a lot of the time, it's OK.	• Make yourself a hot chocolate and drink it slowly. • Ask someone who loves you for a hug. • Give yourself a break from working. • Eat something you love slowly, enjoying every mouthful. • Have a warm bath. • Go for a run. • Talk to someone. • Write a kind letter to yourself pretending you are your best friend and read it often.

Blog Spot

'My mum sometimes says I can be a spiteful cow to her and it hurts. I thought about the idea of a self bully and realised I am a spiteful cow to myself and it hurts me.'

Kaaren, 15

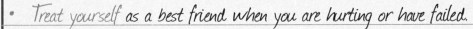

Practice Ideas

- Treat yourself as a best friend when you are hurting or have failed.
- Write a list of things that would make you feel well-treated by yourself: Bath with special bubble bath, read a good novel, watch a funny film, go for a swim, go for a walk or eat something delicious.
- Eat chocolate slowly, tasting every mouthful.
- Each day as you plan, decide three things you will do or say to treat yourself as a friend.
- NOTICE – when you are feeling rubbish and watch when you are mean to yourself with words or actions.
- THEN – BE kind.
- Notice when friends and family say nasty things about themselves like, 'I am fat', 'I am ugly' or 'I am stupid'. Point out to them that being a self bully won't help. Ask them to do the same for you.
- Write 'be kind' on a smooth stone with a permanent ink pen. Put it somewhere you see often to remind you to be kind to yourself.
- When you feel upset, sad or angry, pretend a friend has come to you with the same feelings and situation, and write in your journal what you would do and say to help.
- Look for someone else you can help or make feel good, eg listening to a problem, helping with coursework or giving a compliment.

Shrinking tip 19
Snitch on a smirch: talking about the hard things

For your bag

'Snitching, on a smirch' template

'Don't tell tales. Don't be a grass or a snitch.'

As we grow up these things are said to us frequently by friends, parents and sometimes even teachers. In large organisations like the NHS, police and the government people are now encouraged to 'blow the whistle', to tell someone when people might get hurt or bullied, even when lots of people think what is happening is OK.

Can you be a 'smirch snitch'?

Can you blow the whistle on your smirch? Smirches are bullies but they like their behaviour to stay secret so they don't get caught. Hopefully you can already see that the more you notice their tricky ways, the smaller they seem. As soon as you snitch on them, they shrink away to find someone who will keep quiet and suffer.

Lots of mind troubles start before the age of 14 and often the reason the problems get worse is because young people keep quiet. They suffer the smirch bullying in their head, feeling bad and doing things that are not in line with their values. Instead of snitching they try and get rid of their bad feelings by doing things that please the smirch, like self harm, withdrawing or using food to squash bad feelings.

Your smirch likes you to feel alone and to think you are the only young person who has difficult thoughts and feelings. If you start snitching on the smirch when you are young you can get help and learn how to manage mind problems so they don't get bigger as you get older. We hope that this workbook has helped you to see that you are not alone and that all young people struggle with their mind as they grow up and worry a lot about what others are thinking. If you practise the suggested strategies you will hopefully start to feel better.

NO BULLYING pathetic smirch!

BUT some people have bigger smirches than others...

and need some extra help just like some people in school and college need additional learning support.

You MUST ask for help from a teacher or a doctor if:

- You have thoughts of killing yourself.

- You have panic attacks.

- You are avoiding things you used to do or places you used to go.

- You are cutting yourself, drinking alcohol or taking drugs to block out the pain.

- You feel like life is pointless or not worth living.

- You have problems getting to sleep or staying asleep.

- You don't want to see friends or do things you enjoy.

- You have gained or lost a lot of weight.

- You cry most days.

- You don't care as much about the way you look.

- You feel like you must do certain things like count, wash all the time or repeat things.

- You feel you have no one to talk to.

- You feel worried all the time.

- Someone is doing things to you that make you feel uncomfortable or upset.

The smirch wants you to struggle alone.

So if you are thinking of getting help it will try and stop you with nasty tunes like: *'Everyone else is normal.' 'You are weird and mental.' 'If you tell them, people will lock you up or take you away from your school or family.'*

Can you see these are smirch lies and you need to find some help?

It is great if you have a friend you can tell how you are feeling but often other young people won't know how to help, so ask your friend for support to find an adult you trust. The circles below suggest some ideas for how to ask for help in different ways. See which one suits you best but make sure you snitch on your smirch.

Idea 1:

Start by writing in your journal as that helps you get rid of all your difficult thoughts and feelings without having to think of the right words. You can then use your journal evidence to tell someone. This might be a teacher, a parent or a youth leader. Or you could contact someone who doesn't know you by calling or emailing one of the young people's charities on page 134–135.

Idea 2:

Leave this book open on the right page or read bits out to a trusted adult as a way of starting to talk about what is getting on top of you.

Idea 3:

Write a letter to an adult you trust and explain what you have been thinking and feeling and what helps you.

Idea 4:

Copy and complete the following template and give it to an adult you trust.

Use the template below to help you identify the problems your smirch causes so you can snitch on it!

SNITCHING ON A SMIRCH TEMPLATE

I have these thoughts that are upsetting me:
Eg 'Other people will get hurt.' 'I will fail my exams.' 'I can't cope.' 'I want to die.' 'My body is disgusting.' 'I must check or wash.'

I am having these difficult feelings:
Eg Panic, sadness, anger.

I am doing these things and I want help to stop:
Eg Bullying others, drinking too much, using drugs, skipping school, hurting myself, bingeing or starving myself, crying a lot.

These things are happening to me and I want help to sort them out:
Eg I am being picked on by an adult or peer.
I am being hurt or touched in a way that is upsetting me.
I am being pushed too hard at college or at home.
I am having to give a lot of care to an adult.
My friend is taking drugs or hurting himself.

Shrinking tip 20
Create your own personal shrinking plan

How small is your smirch?

Can you see the things you could do to shrink the power of your smirch? Just reading this workbook is a bit like reading a diet and exercise book and wondering why your body hasn't changed. Shrinking your smirch will require putting into practice the shrinking tips and making some changes to make sure you stay close to your values. This last strategy will help you decide what to do differently so your smirch is as small and weak as it can be.

Let the shrinking begin...

Put here a happy photo of yourself and draw a very small smirch quaking in the corner. It is still there but on your 'struggle days' remind yourself your bag is bigger.

For your bag
Your completed shrinking plan

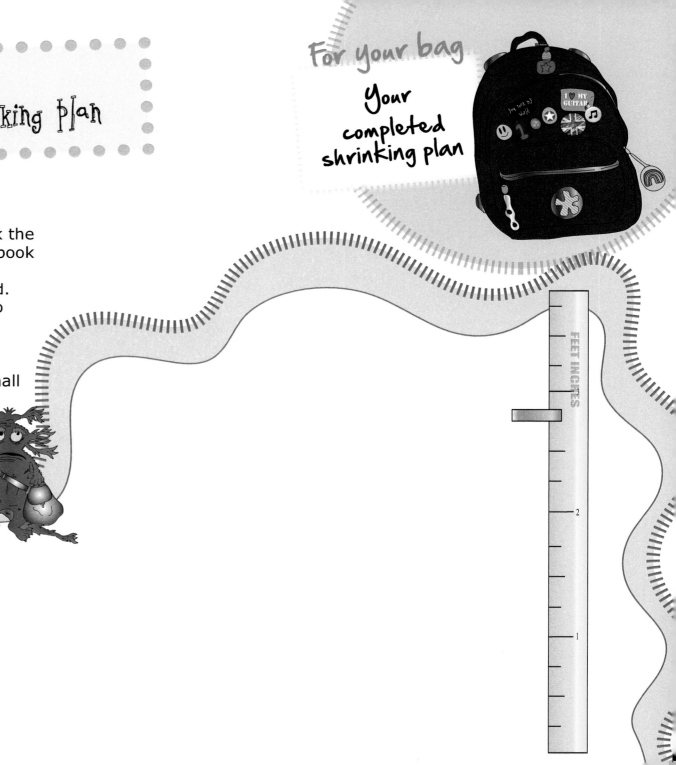

My Shrinking Plan

1

What do I want to be like? What are my values? What things am I going to do however I feel?

....
....
....
....

2

What is my smirch like? What does it look like and what does it make me think, feel and do?

....
....
....
....

3

What am I doing too much and what am I not doing enough?

....
....
....

4

Have I bought a cheerful journal and pen? Add sections for SMART goals, food, mood, planning and movement.

....
....
....

5

When am I going to practise noticing, belly breaths, getting present and STOP? (NO bullying pathetic smirch!)

....
....
....
....

6

What are my smirch's top five tunes? When is the smirchipod on at top volume? What techniques work best to manage my thoughts?

....
....
....
....

7

What feelings do I struggle with most? When do these feelings come up the most often? What techniques can I use to cope better with them?

....
....

8 When in the day will I plan and choose a 'today' goal?

....
....
....
....

9 Write a list of some problems and practise using problem-solving strategies.

....
....
....
....

10 How and when am I going to move more? Can I set a SMART goal to help?

....
....
....
....

14 Can I choose a SMART goal to better manage social media and gaming habits?

....
....
....
....

11 What do I put in my body that makes it feel better or worse? Can I set a SMART goal to make a small step forward?

....
....
....

12 What can I use as a present moment reminder?

....
....
....

13 What are my energy and fatigue patterns? How do my thoughts, feelings and actions change these patterns? Can I set a SMART goal to take more rest?

....
....
....

15 Am I a self bully? Can I start to be kinder in the way I treat myself?

....
....
....

16 How can I grow my gratitude? Can I note 5 good things?

....
....
....

17 Do I need to get some help to shrink my smirch? Check the ideas on page 124 and choose which one you could use to get some adult support.

....

130

CREATE...

...a smirch shrinking life box!

To help you carry on with your smirch shrinking ideas, find a colourful box or decorate a plain one with photos and colours that make you feel happy.

Write each practice tip from this book on to a separate piece of card.

Put all of the cards in your box.

Each day before you leave the house, shake the box so you don't get the same card too often and pick a card without looking. Read it and leave it out until you have done the task.

Write in your journal the things you complete.

As your life changes you can add new cards to keep smirch shrinking for many years.

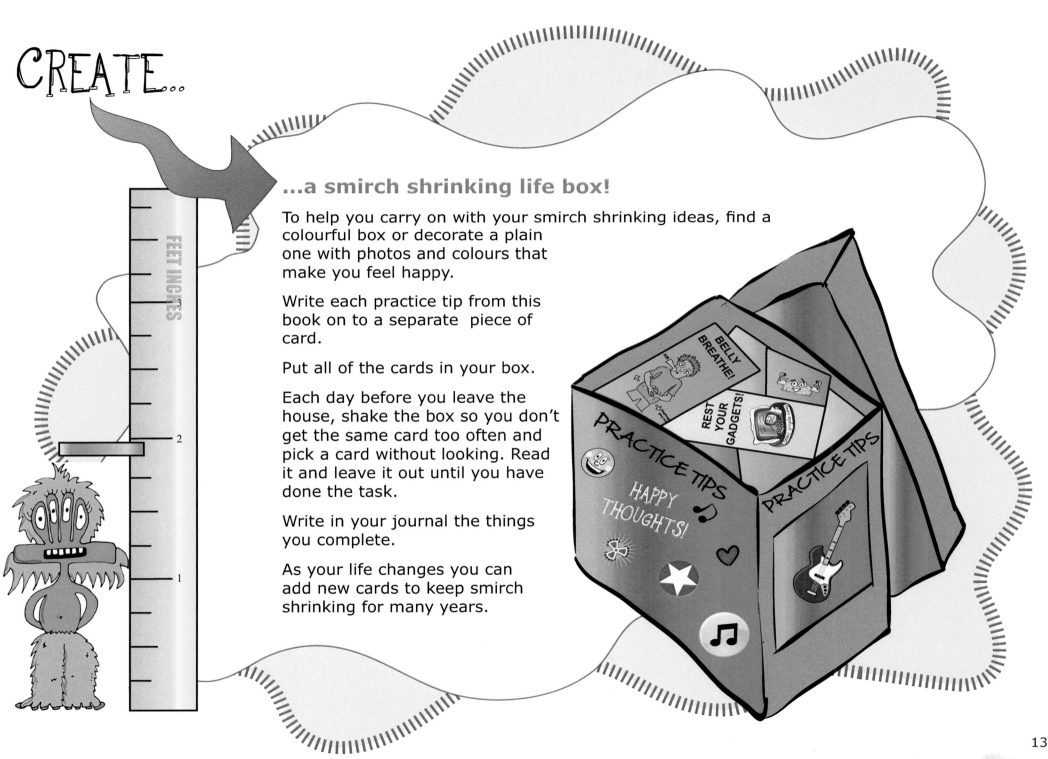

FEET INCHES

3

2

1

Dear Reader

I hope you have found this workbook helpful, I hope your smirch feels less powerful and you feel stronger and more confident to stand up to smirches and smirchins. To get body fit you have to regularly move about and regularly practise specific exercises to make your muscles toned and strong. If you want your mind to get and stay fit you will need to apply the same principles. You need to complete your personal revenge plan, regularly do the smirch shrinking practice ideas and remember your values and how to stay close to them throughout your adult life. It may be helpful to show your personal shrinking plan to friends and family so they can support you to stick with your chosen ideas. You might also want to make a copy of the plan and put it in a place where you can see it often and update it when you achieve your goals and want to make new ones.

If you have found the ideas in this book are helping you, you might start to notice that the adults in your life have quite large smirches and need to do some work too. If they want to, they can buy the adult version of this book by the same title, but you may be able to help them just by talking about the smirch shrinking ways that are helpful to you. Ganging up on the smirch with others works really well.

Make sure you ask for help if your smirch feels like it's growing or simply not shrinking.

Best wishes for the rest of your life. Remember who you want to be.

Jo Johnson

Happy shrinking

A few last words from some young people about their shrinking journey...

'I will definitely carry on with my gratitude diary, it is really helping me feel more positive.'

'I have stopped cutting myself as I have practised present moment stuff (and can now do that), curious scientist experiment and breathing when I feel like cutting. The ice experiment helped me a lot. It took a while though.'

'My confidence is growing, I feel my ideas are as important as other people's so I am not so easily pushed about and made to feel guilty.'

'I have loved making up and shrinking my smirch, I have also worked out, it's not just me, other people feel bad too. Remember it's not just you.'

'Practise planning every day – it really helps to keep you calm.'

Happy shrinking!

Katy, Katie, Jess, Oscar, Mark, Kaaren, Amber, Ruby, Leah, Johanna, Tom, Matthew, Genie, Harriet, Max, Danielle, Dan, Livvy, Hugo, Steed, Sydney, Lauryn, Cerys, Ollie, Sam, Isaac, Owen, James, Nicole, George, Arthur and Dionne

Join the shrinking crew on Facebook!
www.facebook.com/shrinkingthesmirch

1 Childline

ChildLine 0800 1111

Childline is a charity for young people and you can contact them about ANY problem, however small.

How to contact Childline:
Call: 0800 1111
Chat online to counsellors.
ASK SAM a question in the message board.
Email them using the link on the website.
For more information, visit the website below:

www.childline.org.uk

2 Carers Trust

carerstrust
action · help · advice

The Carers Trust gives support to young carers who are looking after someone with a physical or mental health condition.

How to contact the Carers Trust:
Call: 0844 800 4361
Email: support@carers.org
Ask your teacher, GP or librarian for information on your nearest young carers group. Every area should have one. For more information, visit the website below:

www.youngcarers.net

3 Samaritans

SAMARITANS

The Samaritans are an organisation who seek to help those who are finding life hard or those who are feeling very anxious, upset or stressed. They are there 24 hours a day, 365 days a year should you need to contact them.

How to contact Samaritans:
Call: 08457 90 90 90
Email: jo@samaritans.org
For more information, visit the website below:

www.samaritans.org

4 YoungMinds

YOUNGMINDS
The voice for young people's **mental health and wellbeing**

YoungMinds is a charity to help young people stay mentally and emotionally well. The website has lots of information about staying mind fit and what to do if you are worried about your mental health. <u>Headmeds</u> is a website created by young minds about mental health, medication and young people.

How to contact YoungMinds:
Call: 020 7089 5050
Email: ymenquiries@youngminds.org.uk
For more information, visit the website below:

www.youngminds.org.uk

5 Doc Ready

Doc Ready is a website that gives advice about what to expect and how to plan speaking to your Doctor about mental health symptoms. It helps you prepare a checklist of your symptoms to take to your appointment.
Doc Ready is more of an informative website so doesn't have phone/email contact.
However, you can tweet using the contact below:
Twitter: @DocReady
For more information, visit the website below:

www.docready.org

6 Winston's Wish

Winston's Wish
the charity for bereaved children

Winston's Wish is a charity that gives information and support to children and young people who have been bereaved (someone in their family has died).

How to contact Winston's Wish:
Call: 08452 03 04 05 (Mon–Fri 9–5 and Wed 7am–9.30pm)
Email: info@winstonswish.org.uk
For more information, visit the website below:

www.winstonswish.org.uk

7 The Princes Trust

Prince's Trust

The Princes Trust is a charity which offers information and support to young people aged 13-30 who are not in education, training or employment. You can apply online to start a course or get a grant.

How to contact The Princes Trust:
Call: 0800 842 842 or text CALL ME to 07983 385418 to receive a call back within 24 hours.
Email: info@princes-trust.org.uk
For more information, visit the website below:

www.princes-trust.org.uk

Useful apps for staying Mind fit

Friends with Mindi	Moodmaster	Befoodsmart
SMART goals	Anxiety	PsychMeUp
Headspace	Beat panic	CBT4kids toolbox
Being still	Moody me	Smiling Mind
Moodtracker	Mood panda	Safe Spot
Moodkit	Breathe2relax	

The author and illustrator believe that whilst the 20 shrinking tips will improve how you feel about life, the most life-changing smirch-shrinking message is summed up perfectly by Tim Keller in his book *The Reason for God**. He says: 'The only true answer to life's struggles is in the Christian gospel, which is that: I am so flawed that Jesus had to die for me, yet I am so loved and valued that Jesus was glad to die for me.' The New Testament book of John, found in the Bible, is a good place to start if you want more information.

Happy shrinking!

* Keller T (2008) *The Reason for God*, Dutton Penguin Publishers, New York.